dying to do
Letterman
turning someday into today

BY STEVE MAZAN

Health Communications, Inc.
Deerfield Beach, Florida

www.hcibooks.com

Library of Congress Cataloging-in-Publication Data

Mazan, Steve.
  Dying to do Letterman / Steven Mazan.
    p. cm.
  ISBN-13: 978-0-7573-1627-2 (trade paper)
  ISBN-10: 0-7573-1627-1 (trade paper)
  ISBN-13: 978-0-7573-1630-2 (e-book)
  ISBN-10: 0-7573-1630-1 (e-book)
  1. Mazan, Steve—Health.   2. Liver—Cancer—Patients—United States—
Biography.   3. Comedians—United States—Biography.   I. Title.
  RC280.L5M39 2011
  616.99'436—dc23

                                                             2011032365

©2011 Steve Mazan

HCI, its logos, and marks are trademarks of Health Communications, Inc.

Publisher: Health Communications, Inc.
        3201 S.W. 15th Street
        Deerfield Beach, FL 33442–8190

Cover photo by Biagio Messina
Cover design by Larissa Hise Henoch
Interior design and formatting by Lawna Patterson Oldfield

To Howard Stern for his invaluable company on the road,
and Denise for hers at home.

Contents

Introduction 1

1. How to Write One Joke in Two Decades 5
2. Field Day of Dreams 14
3. Growing a Pair: My First Set 19
4. A Not-So-Clean Comedic Start 29
5. Performing at the Wharf 36
6. Impressing Robin Williams 44
7. Out of the Nest 49
8. L.A. Woman 58
9. A Comedy of Errors 74
10. Diagnosis Focus 82
11. In Good Hands 92
12. Reality Sets In 98
13. Message in a Bottle 102
14. My Next-to-Perfect Wedding Day 109

15. That First Year 115

16. With a Little Help from My Friends 119

17. Going Public 129

18. One Step Forward, Two Steps Back 133

19. Back to Basics 139

20. Maybe Baby 148

21. Tom Sawyer 151

22. The Right Tape at the Right Time 156

23. The Letterman List 160

24. Forget the Cutting-Room Floor 169

25. Anticipation 178

26. What Are Friends For? 183

27. Next 185

28. Dying to Do Ferguson? 189

29. On a Roll? 200

30. Small Peaks and Big Valleys: 2008–2009 204

31. So Close 219

32. Finish Line 223

Acknowledgments 251

Introduction

Hello, I'm Steve Mazan. I'm a comedian. Nice to meet you. I hope that introduction wasn't too awkward.

Obviously, what you are holding is a book. But my hope is that what it will really become is a wake-up call. Maybe you can even put it on your bedside stand next to your alarm clock. One will wake you up to your day, and the other to your dreams.

This book tells the story of my own wake-up call. The story of a dream I had since I was a kid, and how I kept hitting the snooze button on that dream because I thought I had plenty of time to reach it.

I never shared my dream with anyone or chased it with all my heart until my wake-up call arrived, blaring at me. But once I started going after it and started telling others about it, an amazing thing happened: people began to tell me that I had inspired them. People I knew my whole life. And people I had never met.

It was obvious I had tapped into something. Most—if not all—of us have some dream we've put on hold or suppressed altogether because the routine of life has taken over. That's just how it goes. But I believe life would be better if we all picked up those dreams, if we all started inspiring one other. Is there any doubt the world would be a better place if it was full of inspired people rather than the uninspired?

The more people I encountered, the more stories I heard about shelved dreams. I wanted to encourage people to reignite their passion and then tell others about it. My own journey taught me that an important part of a dream is sharing it. No dream is reached alone. You either need emotional support or direct help along the way. In most cases, both.

To urge people to share their own dreams, I came up with an idea for a button. A button people could wear that reads, "I'm dying to . . ." and has a blank spot where they could write their goal. A version of the button is on the cover of this very book!

Made ya look! The button on the cover just asks the question, "what are YOU dying to do?" But the ones I hand out to people at shows or screenings of our documentary have a blank where I personally write in what that person is dying to do. To get a button, people have to tell me their dream. I won't hand out blank buttons. I have personalized thousands and thousands of these "I'm dying to . . ." buttons.

Filling them out and hearing people's dreams inspires me. I love it. But the sad thing is, most people don't have an answer for what they want me to write. They have to think about it. Even after waiting in a long line to get the button, they haven't figured it out.

After a minute or two of talking to them and trying to help them figure it out, I let most of them off the hook. I coax a short-term dream out of them like, "I'm dying to drink," "I'm dying to eat pizza," "I'm dying to party," or "I'm dying to see a good movie." And then I give them some homework. I tell each of them they have to go home and think about what they are *really* Dying to Do.

Maybe you picked up this book because you already have a dream in mind. You already know what you are dying to do. Great! Then read on about the incredible things that unfolded once I admitted to myself and everyone around me what I was dying to do, and I chased it with a passion.

If you picked up this book not knowing what it is you are dying to do, I hope you will think about it as you read about my journey. Give it even more focus when you are not reading. Make it your number one priority to answer that question. Not for me, but for you. Fill in that blank.

Knowing what you're dying to do tells you what you are living for.

One note on this. I've met many people along the way who think they've achieved everything they could ever want to accomplish. They tell me they aren't "dying to do" anything. They've got a great life, a great family, a great job. It's as if admitting they have some dream they have ignored is a condemnation of the life they've lived. It's not. You might have reached several dreams in your life—congrats! But old and completed dreams need to be replaced with new ones, otherwise the inspiration goes missing. And we all know what kind of life that leads to: an uninspired life.

I believe this book can really help a lot of people. But it's not set up like a self-help book. There are no lists of what you need to do. No secrets to success. No strategies to implement to change your life. Instead, it's just a story. A bunch of stories that make up my story to date. But I've seen this story inspire people. In fact, the editor of this book, Michele Matrisciani, called me after reading the first draft and told me she was quitting her job. I asked, "Was it that bad?" (I thought I had driven her out of the business!) She told me no, the story was that good. It woke her up. My story had inspired her to finally chase a dream she had: to open her own editing/writing/publishing consulting business. And after helping me edit this book, that is exactly what she did. I was touched, astonished, and inspired right back. Michele admitted what she was dying to do and started chasing it. She filled in that blank.

Now it's *your* turn. Fill in that blank. And read on. Enjoy your wake-up call. And don't even think about reaching for the snooze button.

1

How to Write One Joke in
Two Decades

The first joke I ever wrote was while I was in the Navy. I had told a lot of jokes before then. I had included funny thoughts in stories and reports I did in school. But I had never actually written a joke to tell onstage as a comedian until I was twenty years old.

It's strange. Despite the fact that from the time I was twelve years old I wanted to be a stand-up comedian, I had never attempted to write a joke. To be honest I'm not sure why. Maybe partly because becoming a comedian was my big dream.

I never told anyone I wanted to be a stand-up comic. It would have been silly to share that dream. I know my family would have laughed at me—and although that sounds like a successful beginning to a comedy career, I knew even then that they would be laughing for the wrong reasons.

In a perfect world I would have shared my dream with my mom or dad and they'd say, "Really, Son? You're interested in being an entertainer? Well, let's drive on down to the library and get you some books on writing comedy, and on Monday we'll get you signed up for a theater program for kids."

My parents saying that would have made me laugh. Actually, not just my parents, anyone's parents in my neighborhood. I didn't know anyone involved in stuff like that—show biz. In Hanover Park, the Chicago suburb I grew up in, you played baseball, basketball, and football for the park district until junior high, and then you played for the school. None of my friends were actors or performers. There was no local theater in my town. We put on plays in grade school, but they were the kind where you played a carrot or a dog. No one could build a résumé on that.

The grown-ups in my town were mostly blue-collar workers. My friends' parents were truck drivers, construction workers, carpenters. No one was an entertainer. The closest thing to show biz I knew growing up was my friend Aaron, who lived a couple streets over. His dad was a cameraman for Channel 44, the Chicago UHF station that aired the White Sox games. His dad would tell stories about Harry Caray being drunk in the broadcast booth at Comiskey Park. (That's no mistake. Harry called games for the Sox way before he became a symbol of the Cubs.) A couple of times a year, Aaron's dad would get us tickets to the game, and when the action was dull, he'd find us in the crowd and put us on camera. Hoping that friends from school might see me on TV during the game was as close to getting into show business as I could imagine.

I wanted to be a comedian, but it never felt like a real possibility. I didn't know anyone who was a comedian, so it seemed even sillier than saying I was going to be an astronaut or the president of the United States. At least those were careers teachers would encourage you toward. No one ever said, "If you study really hard and get good grades, you might grow up to be a comic."

In fact the opposite was true. My family laughed all the time. But anytime being funny was mentioned in terms of an occupation or an attribute, it was lambasted. My parents chided my brother, sister, and me for being smart-asses. And somehow my father knew the unemployment figures for people trying to make a living by being funny, because he often answered a smart-ass comment with "Forty thousand out-of-work comedians, and now we have another."

It wasn't in my scope to honestly consider being a comedian as a career choice. And it wasn't in my parents' either. Neither of them went to college, which was their dream for us: get good grades, go to college, and then get a good, stable job you could have the rest of your life. They wanted us kids to have the same life they had, only with better pay and more stability.

So telling my parents I wanted to be a stand-up comedian was never even a consideration. And telling my brother and sister would have only resulted in their laughing at me and then telling my parents, who would have scoffed and joined in on the laughter.

Now, I don't mean to make my family sound awful. They aren't. This is just how we handled everything. We laughed at it. My mom's awful, backbreaking job in a factory? We laughed at it. My teenage brother, Mike, would do a great impersonation of my mom waking up on her one day off, shuffling around in her robe, a cigarette dangling from her mouth, bitching about how she had to work the hardest machine in the building all week. "You kids stay out of my hair today. I've been working number fourteen all week, and the last thing I need is you getting on my nerves, all right?"

This might seem disrespectful, but it wasn't. This portrayal made my mom howl with laughter. Mike would put on the robe, stick an unlit cigarette in his mouth, and nail her demeanor and tone of voice. It made her feel good to laugh, which took away some of the power that job held over her. It helped that his impression was dead on. Even then I knew the value of craftsmanship in comedy.

A better example of laughing to keep from crying was in dealings with my dad. He was a big drinker; he still is. I guess something should be said for sticking with it. I guess he is the Cal Ripken of drinking. My dad is an alcoholic, but as a kid I didn't know that. Strange as it may seem, that word wasn't even used much back then. We'd just say, "That guy is a big drinker." Dad had a job, worked hard, and was seldom sloppy drunk, so it never seemed like a serious problem.

There was a guy who wandered our town, always drunk, in tattered clothes, swearing and mumbling to himself. That guy had a drinking problem. My dad functioned, so it didn't seem serious. Still, he missed a lot of my games, family events, or showed up late and in rough shape. We all wished he would stop, but there was never a thought of rehab or an intervention or any of those other things reality shows are about now. It affected us all. I'm positive seeing him drink influenced a lot of the decisions I made growing up, as well as shaped our family dynamic.

But we didn't sit around feeling sorry for ourselves. We often joked and laughed about it. It was our way of coping. If there was someone on a television show who was drunk or stumbling around, my sister, Cathy, would say, "Dad, I didn't know you were a TV star." We'd all laugh, even my dad. I never asked him, but I think that laughing with us was my father's way of coping with a problem he couldn't kick.

One of our classic family moments was when my dad stumbled into the house while the rest of us were in the living room. I was only six or seven at the time, and my brother and sister were about twelve and thirteen, respectively. The front door flew open and my dad stumbled in and tripped on the doorstep. He tried to right himself but failed miserably, somehow ending up splayed on his back with one leg under him and the other stretched out. Just as we were all about to jump off the couch to see if he was okay, he waved his hands like an umpire and yelled, "Safe!"

We all cracked up—including my dad. It is now a family tradition to yell "Safe!" when anyone, family member or not, takes a fall. Out of a terrible moment, a sad moment, we found some humor.

Laughter didn't take away the sadness or pain of seeing my dad drunk and out of control, but it helped me survive. The alternative was to cry, which we did on many occasions. But crying didn't solve anything. It didn't change anything. And laughing made us at least feel better, like we had some control. We couldn't control the situation, but we could control how we handled it. All that laughing got us through tough times. No matter what, life was going to go on. So we might as well laugh at it.

My point is that if I would have announced to my family that I was planning on becoming a comedian, they all would have laughed at me. I would have laughed at my sister if she'd said she wanted to be an actress. When my brother picked up guitar on his own, we mockingly called him "Nugent." Not because we didn't hope all of one another's dreams would come true, or because we were mean, but because there was so little chance our goals would be reached that it would be an easier letdown if we could laugh about it. If it wasn't taken too seriously, we'd have no reason to feel bad when it didn't happen.

Because I took my dreams to become a comedian seriously, I didn't dare share them with anyone. I wouldn't allow my dream to be scoffed or laughed at. I was so serious, that I didn't even admit to myself that I wanted to be a comedian until I was in my late twenties. I buried my secret ambitions as far as I could, deep down under the sea. Literally.

At eighteen I enlisted in the Navy and served on a submarine as a diesel mechanic, a job I hated. I was proud to serve my country, but the service wasn't the life for me. I didn't like being told what to do all the time. Looking back now, I can appreciate the discipline I gained and the good times I had, but at the time, all I knew was that I didn't want this as a career.

I wasn't a bad sailor. I actually excelled during my time in. I was a hard worker and was assigned to special schools and training. I even got meritoriously promoted by our captain for doing such a great job. I was on a fast track to a successful career, but I planned to get out as soon as my enlistment was up. The Navy has a lot of dedicated men and women in it. But a lot of the ones I met were scoffers, too. They were in the service because it was an easy choice and they wanted to be told what to do; they didn't want to decide for themselves. I did.

Realizing I didn't want to be in the Navy made me start asking myself what I really wanted to do with my life. I was nineteen or twenty. Still years away from admitting to everyone else that I wanted to be a comedian, but I was starting to entertain the possibility to myself. I didn't know how I was gonna do it, but at least I knew what "it" was.

I was living in Newport News, Virginia, and knew of a comedy club in town called Cozzy's Comedy Club. I went there on weekends whenever my sub was in port. I saw a lot of great comics there. Some I remember; most I don't. But seeing comedians live for the first time suddenly made "it" real to me. The dream became attainable. A little less absurd.

The comics seemed like regular people, especially offstage. Onstage they commanded attention and appeared to be the stars they were on television. But when I saw them in the back of the room—by the bar or heading into the bathroom before they went onstage—they seemed just like me. They dressed a little different but didn't come across as untouchable celebrities with so much natural talent and charisma that I could never even consider attempting what they did. They looked and behaved like normal people. Well, except for the fact that they would get up in front of a room full of total strangers and try to make them laugh.

That exception impressed me. Even thinking about walking onto the stage made me nervous. If the comedian talked directly to people in the audience, I would tremble with fear that he might ask me a question. As much as I sensed these comedians weren't too different from me, I wasn't convinced, and I was still too scared to find out. In fact, in the couple of years I attended shows at Cozzy's and observed the comedians on- and offstage, I never once approached one and asked for advice.

That would've been an obvious step, wouldn't it? An easy step? To just gather information? But I was afraid they'd look at me and sneer. They'd tell me I was not like them. I couldn't do what they did. I could have just asked as a curious fan, "How did you get started?" But I was afraid they'd see through me and ridicule me. Then my dream would be out there and crushed before it ever got started.

But while I never approached any of the comedians, I did take notes. Not on paper, because that would have signaled my inter-est to outsiders. I paid very close attention and made mental notes on how the comics moved around the stage, moved their arms, held the microphone. And most of all, I studied how they told their jokes. How they worded them. How they arranged them. How they delivered them.

When I was driving or getting ready for bed, I'd recite their jokes in my head so I could mimic the rhythm and the pacing of the comics I had seen. At some point I told myself I had to try to write my own jokes. I had to put pen to paper to see if I could write a joke that I could see myself, or anyone else, telling.

I was afraid to write everything down in a book. I lived on a submarine, and having anything that resembled a diary or journal would only invite a lot of ribbing. Something like that would most likely be taken from your bunk locker when you weren't looking and passed around the boat behind your back so everyone could read it and join in on the jokes. Instead, I just had a few sheets of loose paper that I kept in a nondescript folder.

I quickly filled up a couple of sheets with joke ideas. Then I worked on editing them until they sounded like something I'd heard at the comedy club. One idea was about the ads on TV where you could feed a kid in Africa for less than the cost of a cup of coffee. My idea was that I didn't have a lot of money, but if I could get in on that cheap food for myself, I could probably afford to help. Another was about a childhood friend's mom who used the word *church* as a verb. As in "You boys need to be churched!" or "Some good churching will get that troublemaking out of you" and how I thought the word "beat" could easily replace "church" in her sentences. Those ideas seemed okay, but I didn't know how to craft them into funny jokes instead of just funny ideas. They weren't ready, so I just filed them in the back of my folder.

But there was one idea I thought was good enough to be told onstage. It sounded to me like any of the jokes I had heard from the professional comedians at the club over the years. I edited it and revised it until I thought it was worded just right. I kept it at the front of my folder as a reminder to myself that I could write a real joke. At some point I worked up the nerve to tell my closest friend in the Navy, Tim O'Neill, that I wanted to be a comic. As expected, he answered with, "Do you have any jokes?"

I told him the joke. He laughed. I can still see his face as he laughed that day. We were at a party later that night and he told his girlfriend the joke I had written. I don't remember if she laughed, but I remember the feeling of pride that someone had passed along a joke I had come up with. I'll never forget it.

I never told that joke onstage. Ever. Even to this day. But if it weren't for that joke, I never would have become a comedian. Here it is:

It's not a great week for my love life. My girlfriend is having her period. I don't know why she calls it a period . . . it's more like an exclamation point . . . but I guess that's better than a question mark.

2

Field Day of Dreams

At least once a week in the Navy we had what was called a "Field Day." This was where all work on the submarine stopped and everyone cleaned. I don't know why they didn't call it "Cleaning Day." I guess it was code so the Russians didn't know we were tidying up. Field Day took place even when we were underway and had been underwater with the hatches closed for weeks. Somehow even in a closed environment, dust and dirt found its way in.

When our submarine, the *Scranton*, was in port, we had lots of inspections by high-level officers who apparently wanted to see their war machine spic-and-span. Even the machinery and engine rooms where I worked had to sparkle. Imagine opening the hood of your car and cleaning the engine every single week. I don't even make my bed that often.

Everyone onboard hated Field Day. It was so monotonous to clean the same thing you cleaned a week earlier. Honestly, most of the four-hour event was spent trying to look busy. It was a relief to get back to some real work when the Chief of the Boat, COB, announced over the speaker, "End Field Day."

Because I worked in the engine room, one of the dirtier areas of the submarine, shipmates who worked elsewhere were assigned to come down and help my division. One of those guys who always came to my workspace was Quartermaster Jeff Paige. Jeff worked in the control room, charting the boat's course. His workspace consisted of a couple of tables where they laid out the maps. It took about two minutes to wipe down his area—if you milked it. So Jeff would inevitably be sent down to help us.

Jeff and I became great friends. When he came down to clean, he'd find out where I was and pretend to be cleaning something nearby. And then we'd spend the next four hours cracking each other up with stories, jokes, and complaints.

One Field Day we started fantasizing about what we would be doing in a couple years when we both got out of the Navy. At first we joked about sleeping in, eating good food, and never having a Field Day. But at some point amid the laughter, I felt like I could tell Jeff what I really wanted to do. I made a couple more jokes and then nervously said, "You know what I really want to do?"

I sensed Jeff could tell I was being serious. He got serious, too. "What?"

"I wanna be a stand-up comic."

Jeff smiled big. "Of course. You'd be great, man. You crack everyone up." Then he added, "Not me, but everyone else."

We laughed and then he continued. "You know what I'm gonna do?"

I could tell he wasn't joking anymore. "What?"

"I'm gonna be twenty-two when I get out. I'm gonna take my G.I. Bill and go to the best school I can and walk onto their baseball team. I'm good, Steve. But I didn't take it seriously in high school. I will now. I'm gonna play pro ball someday."

I believed him. Jeff wasn't a bragger.

Jeff and I started hanging out a lot when we were on liberty (off work). He was from Iowa, so we shared a Midwestern sensibility of working hard and playing hard. We both loved playing basketball, softball, and video games. He was one of those guys who was good at everything. But he wasn't cocky, so you didn't resent it. He was a good-looking guy, too. He had a warm smile that girls loved. My wife at the time, Kathy, told me that when all the wives and girlfriends talked, Jeff was singled out as the guy on the boat they all thought was cutest. There was never any mention of me being on that list. I'm sure this was an oversight.

Jeff died in a car crash while he was home on leave a year before he was scheduled to get out. I heard the news while I was at work on the sub. Some guy new to the boat told me he had just heard a couple guys talking about it. I thought it must be some kind of joke. Most jokes in the Navy were sick, so this wouldn't be too far of a stretch. But the punch line never came. I went right to the control room, where Jeff's division was, and confirmed the news.

I didn't cry. I couldn't. It was more like I felt nothing at all. Like I was dead inside. It felt surreal. No one close to me had ever died. My grandparents were all dead before I was born. I knew I was supposed to cry, but I couldn't. I just felt stunned.

The Chief of the Boat announced that the *Scranton* would be sending four representatives to attend Jeff's funeral in Iowa. The four were another Quartermaster from his division and Jeff's three roommates. I immediately went to the COB and told him I needed to go.

"No." The COB explained that these chosen people would represent the command.

"I don't want to represent the command; I want to represent me. I need to go."

"No." He turned and walked away.

I went right to the chief of my division and told him I wanted leave to go to the funeral. He said to me that a group was already being sent. Again I expressed my need to go and I wanted him to approve my leave. He refused, saying he couldn't afford to have me gone right then. I pleaded with him about how much more important it was for me to go than it was for him to have me there. Again, he refused my request.

The group was leaving the next day. I told Tim O'Neill, my friend and one of Jeff's roommates, that I was going to go with them and asked where to meet them. He said they were leaving from the *Scranton* at 8:00 AM the next morning.

So I arrived at the ship in civilian clothes. Both my chief and the COB saw me standing on the pier, obviously not heading to work. They both chewed me out and warned me about all the trouble I would be in if I didn't get on the boat. They said I would be considered AWOL. I told them I didn't care, I had to go. Of course, I did care. I just cared more about going to Iowa and saying good-bye to Jeff. I had never disobeyed an order till that day, and I understood the severity of what I was planning. Being Absent Without Leave was a serious offense. But I knew that moment meant more than the remaining two years of my naval career.

I also had an ace up my sleeve. I was the only diesel tech onboard, and one of two oxygen generator operators. The ship could not go to sea without at least one of both those positions onboard. The other oxygen generator operator was scheduled to be in school when we got underway in a couple weeks. So if they reported me AWOL, I would be arrested upon my return and miss that trip. They'd have to scramble to fill my two positions, pulling guys from another sub. They couldn't afford to do that. And I knew it.

A few minutes before we took off for Iowa, my chief came up on the pier and told me that they were granting me five days leave. He told me that both he and the COB were pissed. And that when I got back, he'd bust my hump. Then he put his arm on my shoulder, squeezed it, and said, "Drive safe." I knew he understood. He did bust my ass with extra work when I got back, but he also started treating me with a new respect.

I didn't cry at the funeral either. I still felt empty. On the twenty-hour drive back to Virginia from the funeral, all I thought about was Jeff. I tried to remember all the good memories we had. There were way too many, even for that long ride. But one pivotal memory popped up while driving on a dark stretch of Indiana highway. No one in the car had spoken for a while when I recalled the Field Day when Jeff dreamed of playing in the majors and I dreamed of doing comedy. Jeff would never get to play pro baseball now. I wondered if I would really become a comedian.

I knew the answer. Because Jeff couldn't chase his dream, I had to. I owed it to him. The memory of that Field Day stuck with me all through that night. And much longer.

3
Growing a Pair: My First Set

As soon as my time in the Navy was up, I got out. The captain of my boat and several of the senior officers tried to get me to re-enlist. I had never had a one-on-one meeting with the commanding officer or his second in command, the executive officer (XO), until I announced I was leaving. Then I was called to both of their staterooms, and behind closed doors, they repeatedly told me that the best decision I could make would be to stay in the Navy. Both the captain and the XO expressed that I was making a mistake not to re-enlist. They said that life in the civilian world was tough and I shouldn't be jumping into it. They warned that jobs were scarce and it would be very hard to make a living in the "real world." They asked me what I thought I was going to do.

Well, at this point, I had told only a couple of my close friends my goal of becoming a comedian. Sharing that with two high-ranking naval officers who were already pooh-poohing my plans didn't sound like a good idea. Can you imagine the conversation if I'd told them my long-term plans?

CAPTAIN: You know, Petty Officer Mazan, it's a very unsafe time to head out into the real world. There's lots of educated and well-trained people fighting for very few jobs. The Navy offers you a very stable place to continue your life; a steady paycheck and a clear direction. What career do you see yourself in?

ME: Well, Captain, I was thinking of becoming a stand-up comedian.

CAPTAIN: Ha ha ha. No, seriously.

ME: Oh, no sir, I'm serious.

CAPTAIN: What? You've got to be kidding. Do you know how many unemployed comedians there are?

ME: My dad says about forty thousand.

The last thing I would do was share my crazy dream with the people trying to get me to stay in the Navy. So I just said that I was "going to college, using my G.I. Bill." That wasn't a lie. I knew I couldn't walk right off my sub and into a comedy club for a paycheck. It would take time.

Also, my favorite comedians were all very smart and educated. I don't mean they had a lot of degrees or went to great schools. I had no idea if they did. What I mean is they knew a lot. They seemed well-read, worldly. They kept up on current events and knew their history. The comedians I liked took the stage with authority and confidence, and I think a lot of it came from feeling like they knew what they were talking about. So I was going to go to college and study communications, literature, and history, while simultaneously learning the comedy ropes.

I am still amazed at how negative and pushy these high-ranking officers were when I told them my college plans. The captain said my G.I. Bill would be there in four more years, when the economy was stronger and jobs more plentiful.

"But if I wait, I'll miss those opportunities because I would just be starting school, rather than finishing it," I answered.

By the way, this was mid 1990, and a peek at the history books will tell you that the late '90s was one of the golden ages of economic growth. Not that I knew that at the time. My point is these officers didn't know it at the time either. But instead of offering me a slew of advantages to staying in the Navy, they gave me every reason not to go into the civilian world. They basically tried to scare me into staying. I didn't take it personally. These men, as powerful as they were, had even higher-ranking people to answer to. They had retention rates to worry about and numbers to hit. But that's what amazed me: anytime someone planned to get out, they received this same alarming sales pitch.

Honestly, it wasn't an easy pitch to ignore. When I first made the decision to get out, I was confident it was the right choice. But after each meeting, I was less and less so. Had I been a less stubborn person, I might have changed my mind.

I guess I should have been ready for this. I do a joke when I perform for the troops where I say that serving in the armed forces is a lot like prison. Everyone talks about how much time they've served; how much time they have left. And what bad decisions led them there. All the troops, Army, Navy, Marines, and Air Force love this joke. Because it's true.

The service isn't what you see in a war movie. Or a commercial. It's a lot less exciting. It's honorable, but, for the most part, pretty routine. So a lot of time is spent commiserating with the other people you are serving with. Nine out of ten guys I worked with in the Navy were counting down the days until their enlistment ended. When you reached the final months of your enlistment, everyone started calling you a "short-timer." Everyone envied the short-timers. Everyone looked forward to being in those shoes.

But an amazing thing happened almost every time. These short-timers almost always re-enlisted! Even though they had been counting down the days to getting out. Even though they had shared their dreams of moving back home to their old friends and family. Even though they had told everyone that a year from now they'd be doing whatever job it was they had dreamed about in their bunks at night.

That's why I shouldn't have been surprised by the tactics used in my meetings with my chain of command. It should have been obvious that there was some incredible salesmanship going on. Some pitch that turned these confident short-timers into "lifers." I guess even if I had prepped myself for the hard sell, I wouldn't have been ready. I would have expected the kitchen sink of offers to be thrown my way: a bonus, a promise of more specialized schooling, and above all, a serious description of the honor and glory in continuing to serve my country. Instead, I got a frightening depiction of how bad my life would be if I left the Navy.

As I said, it almost worked. But then I realized it wasn't personal. Everyone was getting scared into staying. By and large, the people who re-enlisted after years of saying they were getting out were just scared. That's who comprised the career-level positions in the Navy—men and women who were too scared to chase anything else.

Don't get me wrong. Many men and women are in the service because they want to be there. They dreamed of a career in one of the branches. But from my experience, I think they are the minority.

This isn't a condemnation of anyone serving our country for a living. Even if they are doing it for stability. They are no different from my parents. They value security above all else. My shipmates who re-enlisted are no different from people who work in an office job they hate but never do anything about it. For me, this was my first lesson on how a lot of adult life worked. I decided I wasn't going to make any life decisions based on fear. I was only twenty-three, but I knew life was too short to live like that.

So in May of 1994, I crossed the gangplank of the USS *Scranton* for the last time. I was scared. Scared of what lay ahead. But even more scared of continuing to waste time doing something I knew wasn't for me. As I left the ship, as is tradition, the guard on watch announced over the ship's P.A. system, "Machinist Mate, Second Class, Steve Mazan, departing."

I've heard a lot of stories and seen a lot of movies where people walk out doors or drive away and never look back. I didn't do that. I looked at the submarine I had served on for over four years the whole time I walked away. One last time I drove around the base I had lived on. Almost immediately, all the reasons I didn't like the Navy washed away. Those reasons gave way to all the good memories I had. The bad times, the rough times: they were put way in the back of my mind. I moved forward with pride for my service and warmth for all the friends I had made along the way.

I had been accepted at Northern Illinois University, a state college about an hour from my hometown. It was close to my family and old friends, but far enough that I would have to move there with my wife, Kathy.

I didn't go straight to college. I spent the summer of '94 hanging out with my wife and friends, and seeing my family for the longest stretch of time since I had lived with them years earlier. I also started learning a new skill—bartending. Even with the G.I. Bill paying for my tuition, Kathy and I would need money to live on. I would have to get a job once I went away to school.

Tending bar seemed like a logical choice. I spent plenty of time drinking in the Navy. Sailors have a reputation to live up to, and I did my part. If they gave medals for drinking, I think my uniform would have been covered with them. A Purple Liver maybe.

Whenever our ship pulled into port, we took over the nearest drinking establishment. After weeks underwater with the same smelly guys, a few cold beers chased away all the stress. We'd take in the culture and sights the following day. Hungover. That's probably why I remember Europe being so out of focus.

Although I was a talented drinker, I was cautious of ending up in the same state as my father. I didn't want to become dependent on alcohol. I never brought beer home to keep in the fridge. For me, drinking was for celebrating and having a good time. Not for routine or getting through the day.

Another factor in my becoming a bartender was that it ran in my family. Before I was born, my grandfather had owned a popular bar in Chicago. While growing up, my father lived above the bar. I'm sure this was the early influence of alcohol in his life. A couple of my uncles owned bars in the city when I was a kid. My dad and I would stop in and say hello whenever we were in the neighborhood. I don't recall ever seeing either of my uncles outside of their bars.

I grew up in bars. Besides visiting my uncles' taverns, my father regularly stopped in bars when I was with him. My dad knew bars wherever we went. If Fodor's had decided to publish a book about Drinking Establishments of the Midwest, my dad could have written it from memory. Somehow he knew the bartenders at every one. As a kid I thought my dad just knew everyone. But at some point it hit me that he didn't know anyone at K-Mart or other stores, just at bars. It was still pretty impressive.

This probably all sounds very wrong, and it was. But I didn't know any different. Bars were fun places. No other kids were ever at the bars—except maybe my brother. But I always got a soda, some peanuts, and if they had it, a candy bar. Most bars at that time had a pinball machine. My dad would feed me quarters. The guys hanging around would feed me quarters, too. And as long as I had quarters and soda, I was satisfied.

One of my earliest memories is of our neighborhood bar, The Hanover Tap. That place was my dad's second home. And, as such, I spent a lot of time there, too. My dad would stop there on the way home from work every day, as did most of the people in the bar. I remember being in The Tap many times when the phone would ring. Before the first ring stopped, five or six guys yelled at the bartender, "I'm not here!" It was pretty funny to see the bartender scanning the faces to see who was admitting they were there and who was denying it.

My dad must have felt bad about lying to my mom in front of me, because instead of saying, "I'm not here," like everyone else, he would say, "I just left." It was obvious to me that my dad had not in fact "just left," but if it was my mom on the phone, we would leave right away. By right away I mean after he finished his beer.

So I felt extremely comfortable in bars. Bartending became an obvious choice for a part-time job, especially since I would be moving to a college town. I'd have plenty of options. But I had no experience. Fixing engines on submarines didn't really qualify me for tending bar. And my award-worthy career on the customer side of the bar wouldn't impress employers. Plenty of people had that résumé.

So I decided to fill the summer before college started by getting some on-the-job training. As luck would have it, my dad had recently retired from his glass-installing career and started tending bar part-time at his old haunt, The Hanover Tap. My parents had divorced when I was about ten years old, and a few years later Dad started dating The Tap's owner, Barb, a great lady. My dad dating a tavern owner is like Scooby-Doo dating the Scooby-snack maker.

Dad and Barb are still together today. She has become family, sharing holidays and trips. We often joke that if they ever broke up, we would really miss my dad. Barb was extremely generous that summer and allowed me to come in and learn the trade by working with my dad. After a couple of weeks, I started filling in for other bartenders. By the end of the summer, I was as comfortable behind the bar as I had been in front of it.

In August, Kathy and I rented a one-bedroom apartment at the university. We were right next to the football stadium. The roar of the crowd and thousands of people milling about before and after games was exciting. The campus full of young men and women was a far cry from the years I spent on the submarine. In the Navy, my days were regimented and routine. At school, I had no one to answer to except myself. The professors didn't care if I was there or not. I don't think I could have handled all that freedom if I had gone to college right out of high school.

Luckily, there was a bar right near my apartment complex called The Stadium Club. Because the football season was in full swing, the bar was busy, and the owner was looking for help. So my showing up looking for a job was perfect timing. I started my first real bartending job within a week of arriving in town.

I was having a lot of fun working and had even more fun at college. I was a few years older than most of the students, but I loved the college lifestyle. Even the learning! I had never enjoyed school growing up. But now that I was taking courses I had a real interest in, I loved it. I also enjoyed the social aspect—the parties, the events, the staying out late. But that lifestyle started shining a bright light on the cracks in my marriage.

Kathy and I started having problems during my last year in the Navy, and we had discussed on a few occasions how things had to change. Because I was gone so much in the Navy, Kathy and I had to get reacquainted every time I came home after months at sea.

Despite all the time apart, we never cheated on each other. We told ourselves and each other that whatever difficulties we had would be solved by getting out of the Navy and having more time together. We were wrong. All the time apart had made us both independent. Living together every day tested that independence.

I wanted to stay out late and party at the bar after it closed. Kathy wanted me home. She wanted to start a family. My idea was to get through college and start doing comedy. Getting into comedy didn't sound like a very probable plan if there were babies to feed. It seemed much more likely that I'd feel pressured to get a nine-to-five job to support them.

By the time my first semester had ended and Christmas rolled around, Kathy and I were separated. At the time it was obvious to both of us that we had grown into people who wanted different things. It had happened over the years in the Navy, but we never really had enough time together to discover ourselves as a couple. We met in high school and dated for three years before getting married at the age of twenty. Now, in our mid-twenties, we were headed in opposite directions.

Kathy moved out of our apartment when I was in class one day. As much as I knew we were doing the right thing, it felt awful. I loved Kathy. But I learned that you need more than just love to make a relationship work. You need to share a direction for your lives. We didn't have that. Kathy wanted a family and deserved one. But if I was going to live my dream, I wouldn't be able to give her what she wanted for a long time. If I started a family and got a real job I'd resent her, and if she postponed having babies so I could chase comedy she'd resent me.

Kathy and I saw each other for a few more months but were divorced within a year. We lost touch pretty quickly. Neither of us wished ill toward the other, so it wasn't messy, but still it was too hard to stay friends.

To this day Kathy was one of the kindest people I have ever met. She taught me a lot about how to treat people. Even as we were splitting up she remained incredibly supportive to me. One time she came home and caught me telling jokes into a tape recorder. She asked to hear it. I was a bit insecure but knew she was someone I could share with. I rewound the tape then hit PLAY. After each joke I told on the tape there was a slight pause and then a big audience roar that began and ended quickly. Kathy surmised that I had recorded laughter and applause from TV shows in between each joke. We laughed at both the silliness and inventiveness of it. It's probably one of the last great moments we shared. Incredibly, she could share laughter and be supportive about what was one of the main reasons we were breaking up.

That tape recorder was the first time I told a bunch of jokes at once. It was my first set. The audience was imaginary; the laugh track was taken off a rerun of *The Jeffersons*. I was still five years away from a real audience. But I would play that tape to myself when I was alone, listening to jokes I had written. That I was delivering. And even with fake laughter, it felt like a real step forward.

4

A Not-So-Clean Comedic Start

College didn't get me any closer to stand-up comedy. It made me better once I started, but it didn't get me doing it. I'm sure the history courses helped give me some perspective and a world view. I also took a lot of literature and creative writing classes. That definitely made me a better writer. But I was writing essays and short stories, not jokes.

My ultimate goal still found a way to creep into my coursework. One assignment for a writing class was to bring a sample of what I thought great writing was. Other students read passages of Twain, Faulkner, and Shakespeare. I read from *David Letterman's Book of Top Ten Lists*. Everyone exchanged strange looks when I announced my selection. I still remember the list I read:

Top Ten Things Overheard
in Line for *Kickboxer II*

#10 I hear there's lots of kickboxing in this one.

#9 If you didn't see part one, you won't be able to follow it.

#8 It's a lot like Star Wars—only it doesn't take place in space and there's a lot more kicking.

#7 Do me a favor and kick me a couple times to get me in the mood.

#6 Excuse me, Mrs. Onassis—but could you quit shoving?

#5 I'll bet Julia Roberts broke up with Kiefer Sutherland 'cause he couldn't kickbox.

#4 So after I knocked over the vase and flowers, my Mom said, "No more kickboxing."

#3 Aaieee! Killer bees!

#2 Do you think Kickboxer could beat Terminator?

#1 It's the best movie ever made about people kicking each other.

I finished reading the list aloud without anyone laughing, not even a chuckle. The most I heard was someone shifting uncomfortably in his chair. When I finished, the professor gave me a nod and we went on to the next student, who read something from *The Great Gatsby*.

I felt like an idiot, but at least it was over, or so I thought. Later some snooty guy across the room asked if I really thought a Top Ten List belonged in this class.

"Yeah, definitely," I said. "It's not the great American novel, but it's creative, clever, and, above all, hilarious. It makes a lot of people laugh; that's a good thing."

Someone else asked, "Just because it's popular, does that make it great?"

"No," I replied, "but popularity doesn't make it not great."

Then a girl chimed in. "I don't find any of it terribly clever."

"How could you not laugh at 'I hear there's lots of kickboxing in this one'?" I argued.

I got a lot of stares. The professor suggested we move on.

I obviously didn't have too much in common with the people in that class, so I decided to not become an English major. Instead, I chose communications and media studies, since classes in that major were more relevant to what I wanted to do in the future anyway. Communications and media studies required me to do a lot of broadcasting at the campus TV station and participate in making a short movie my senior year. I did a few internships at ABC stations in Chicago and Rockford. I learned to run cameras and do a lot of behind-the-scenes production.

Northern Illinois University is in a small farm town with no place to do comedy. I worked the weekends bartending, so I didn't have time to go into Chicago even to see a comedy show. I had put my dream on the back burner. By the time I graduated, I was planning to do promotions for a radio or television station to make ends meet.

The way broadcasting works, whether you are reporter, producer, director, or promotions person, you start in a small market. For example, you work in Buffalo till you are good enough to move to a mid-sized market like Indianapolis. Then you strive to break into one of the big markets like New York or Chicago.

Well, I moved to San Francisco after college to be closer to my sister, who was living there with her family. Having only older siblings, I was excited to be able to see my niece and nephew grow up. But the San Francisco Bay Area was the fifth biggest broadcasting market at the time and not exactly the place to break in. It was a bad move for a fledgling broadcasting career. I ended up bartending at a sketchy dive bar.

Luckily it was 1999, and there was something big going on in the Bay Area—the dot-com boom. New companies were starting every day. And they were staffing like crazy. That's how I landed my first office job at a staffing company, Sterling Personnel. It was a small agency with a couple of great women who owned and ran the company. Having women as my bosses was different from my years in the Navy, and it took a while to get used to it. But once I did, I loved it. These weren't just great business women, they were great people. I learned a lot from them. And I made some great money.

Unfortunately, by the end of my first year in the Bay, my sister's husband, Sam, got a job back in Chicago, so they all moved away. I had moved across the country for them, and they moved to where I had come from. I wasn't sure if that was sad or funny. I did know that I was left alone. I toyed with the idea of going back, too.

Two things kept me in the Bay. I had a great job. And I had recently learned that San Francisco had one of the best comedy scenes in the country. So I decided to stay. I told myself that if I was going to be on my own, almost two thousand miles from my family and friends, it was time to finally take a real step toward becoming a comedian.

I immediately started searching online for comedy clubs and open mics. I came across a guy who said he coached people who were trying to become comics. I got excited. This seemed like a perfect way to start—by learning all about it from an expert. I was still in my student mode from college, so taking a comedy course seemed like a no-brainer. Now I'd have someone to ask all the questions I was afraid to ask the comedians I had seen.

I signed up right away. It was an expensive eight-week course of one-on-one training. The first few weeks were great. I learned so much about how the business works and how to structure jokes and discipline myself to write material. I learned that the first big step was to get a five-minute set together. Open mics and clubs gave new comics five minutes of stage time, so developing the set was crucial.

After four weeks I had put together my first five-minute set. I was so excited. I practiced it over and over on the drive to and from work. But the coach kept discouraging me from going to an open mic. He said I should wait. Then he started pushing for me to sign up for another eight weeks of classes. It became obvious that as valuable as this class might be, the coach was trying to slow me down so I'd need him (and pay him) longer.

Finally, after six weeks I told him I was done waiting. I was going to attend open mics. He advised against it. I found out about a comedy show at a place called The Brainwash Café, a coffee shop in the middle of a Laundromat. I swear. You performed for people while they folded their clothes.

I showed up at 7:00 PM for what was advertised as an 8:00 PM show. I added my name to the sign-up sheet, for the tenth spot. I figured with five-minute sets, I would get up around 9:00. That would give me time to watch for a bit and get over my nerves. This was a Wednesday and I had to work the next morning, so I didn't want to go much later. The guy who ran the show didn't show up until about 8:45. Close to thirty comics had signed up and were waiting. I felt out of place. My coach had told me to dress nice, so I wore a dress shirt and sports jacket. No one else was wearing anything remotely dressy. Most of the comics were wearing T-shirts. Some even looked homeless.

The show finally started just before 9:00 PM, and the host, Tony Sparks, did about fifteen minutes of material. He was a super-nice black guy, and everyone seemed to love him. He didn't really tell any jokes; instead he just talked and laughed at himself. None of the comics after him did five minutes. Most did between seven and ten. So when the tenth spot that I had signed up for came around it was already going on 10:30.

For some reason, Tony didn't call my name for the tenth spot. I figured maybe I'd counted wrong and waited for the next introduction. Not me. Not the twelfth, either. I was nervous for so many reasons, and now I felt even worse that I didn't know what was going on. I worked up the nerve to talk to Tony while the thirteenth comedian was on.

Tony asked if I was new. He said that a lot of veteran comics pop in and he puts them up if he can. So the order doesn't match up exactly to the list. He told me to wait in the back and he'd find me right before I was going up so he could get my introduction.

An introduction? I hadn't even thought about that. I went to the back of the Laundromat and started thinking about how I wanted Tony to bring me up. After a few more comics had gone up, I had the introduction down. Simply, "This guy is originally from Chicago, please welcome Steve Mazan."

I looked for Tony, but he was outside with other comics who had already gone on. When he came back in, at a little after eleven, we made eye contact and he gave me a nod that I somehow understood as "soon."

At about 11:45 the guy working the café part of the business yelled, "Last call," and then told the people in the Laundromat to wrap up. I was so confused. I finally went back up to Tony and asked what was going on. He said he wasn't sure if they'd have time to get to me tonight. Because this was my first time meeting Tony, and anyone involved in the San Francisco comedy scene whatsoever, I did my best to control my temper. I had been nervous all week about this night. All day I had grown even more nervous. It kept building and building as I waited in the Brain-wash for the show to begin. Once other comics started perform-ing, I really got anxious. I was so tense by the time Tony told me I might not go up that I didn't know if I was going to yell or cry.

I think Tony sensed this. He said, "All right, good friend, I'll get you up in two more. I'm not sure if it will be five minutes, because we gotta be outta here at midnight, but I'll get you up."

I gulped and nodded my approval. Ten minutes later, Tony brought me up. Four people were left in the building: Tony, the comic before me, the café worker, who was now sweeping the floor, and me. I rambled so fast that I got my entire five minutes out in three. Tony made everyone give me a big round of applause because it was my first time. The comic before me said he liked one of my jokes.

Everything about the night had been awful. The location, the set-up, the sound, the lights, my delivery, the response: all were as bad as possible. But when I left that laundromat I was on top of the world. I felt like I had helium in my head. I floated to my car. It was after midnight, and I had an hour's drive home. On the drive, I relived every horrible moment of the night in my head over and over. As I crossed the Bay Bridge, leaving San Francisco behind, I broke into a smile, punched the roof of my car, and screamed as loud as I could.

"Wooo-hoooo!" I had done stand-up comedy.

5

Performing at the Wharf

Starting comedy is a bit of a catch-22. The only way to get better is to get as much stage time as possible. The problem is the only way to get bookers to give you stage time is to be a good comic. A lot of people looking for a real job after college run into this problem, but they have the option of an internship. There are no internships in stand-up.

Imagine seeing a comedian onstage and a couple feet behind him is another guy taking notes. After a few jokes, the main comic waves the new comic forward and they switch places. The intern-comic attempts a few jokes, looking back over his shoulder every couple seconds to see what the pro thinks. The real comic offers advice. "No, no, no. Remember: set-up then punch line. Not the other way around."

I don't think audiences would sit through that. So beginning comics try to get stage time wherever possible. You try to get on showcases at the comedy clubs and booked shows at bars that have comedy nights. But there are probably only twenty spots available a week in any city for new comics and a hundred newbies trying to get them. If you're lucky, you might get two of those spots on a good week.

Two sets a week will not help you get better at comedy. There is such a learning curve when you start that you need to get onstage, do your act, and then with the lessons from that set fresh in mind, get back onstage. To get good quickly, you need to get up at least once a night—at least. Since that is impossible at any quality booked show, new comics with any hustle do open mics.

Open mics are comedy shows at bars, coffee houses, and other random places (see Laundromats). Usually the patrons at these places have no idea a comedy event is about to happen. You're competing with people watching a ballgame or reading a book. They're often mad that you are talking over what they came out to do. Open mics are awful for comedy. But they are great for learning. You don't have to be booked at these shows. Just show up, sign up, and perform.

When I started, I would get in a minimum of ten sets a week. That was with a forty-hour-a-week day job and an hour commute each way. I was determined to get good. I didn't consider it work; I loved it. I did every open mic possible every night. Some weeks I got over twenty sets in. Sometimes I'd drive into San Francisco after work, do a five-minute set at an abandoned luggage store, and then drive fifty miles to San Jose to do another five at a dive bar. I'd practice my new jokes the whole way. I was getting better. I felt more comfortable onstage. I was finding out which jokes worked and which didn't. (There were a lot more jokes that didn't.)

After the last open mic of the night, I'd often go to a diner and hang out with other new comics. We'd share tips and battle stories. We'd tell each other which open mics were the best and which weren't worth traveling to. This was also where you'd make a connection for getting onto one of the booked shows in the area. The real shows, with real audiences.

One night I was at Denny's with a couple of comics, Drennon Davis and Mark Nadeau. We were commiserating about how hard it was to get in front of real, captive audiences. None of us were getting sets at the actual clubs. We thought about starting our own shows at our own location, but that would take a lot of work and promoting. It would take our focus off the stage time. And who knew if we could get an audience anyway. Drennon wished there was a way to capitalize on a place where people were already gathered. Mark agreed that there had to be some group of people we could convince to come and see us do comedy. And that's when I came up with one of the worst ideas of my life.

"What if we take the comedy show to that group?" I said.

"Huh?" Mark and Drennon responded in unison.

"Why don't we find out where there is a large group waiting around for something, and do comedy while they wait?"

They were both intrigued.

"Like where?" Mark asked.

"The Wharf," I said.

San Francisco is a beautiful city. The minute I moved there, I had friends and family from all over the country coming to visit me. In less than a year I had been to Alcatraz three times. One more visit and I'd get my own cell. Alcatraz and a lot of other San Francisco landmarks are just off of Fisherman's Wharf, where there are always lines of hundreds of people waiting for the tour boat, bus, or ferry. These people were captive. They couldn't leave. They were bored. Why not try to do some comedy for them?

Mark and Drennon immediately thought it was a genius idea.

That should have been a sign, but it didn't register. We all figured this was a no-brainer. Lots of street performers were already at the Wharf: Magicians. Jugglers. Mimes. Even guys who just painted themselves silver and stood still. But no comedians.

We would be breaking new ground. We'd be entertaining the masses. There would be a new line every hour. We could get several sets in one location. We'd be giving laughter to people tired of standing in line. And we'd do it for free. Heck, the tours they were in line for would probably thank us. How come nobody else had ever thought of this?

Well, nobody else thought of it because it was a stupid idea. That Saturday (the busiest tourist day), Mark, Drennon, and I showed up at a bustling Fisherman's Wharf. Drennon brought a mic, amp, and extension cord. It was summer in San Francisco, so it was freezing. On top of that, the wind was extra strong.

We found a huge line of people waiting for a boat to Alcatraz. Perfect. There were easily 200 tourists in line, all zig-zagged and bunched up, so they looked like a real audience rather than a line. Drennon found an electrical outlet in the cement that a Churro cart was using. The Churro girl looked suspicious and angry when we asked if we could share the outlet. I guess I'd be angry, too, if I were a Churro girl. She didn't answer either way, so Drennon plugged in.

Next to the line of people was a three-foot high cement mooring bollard where ships must have tied up years ago. It was wide enough to stand on. But not to move around on—just to stand very still on. This would be our stage. With the stiff wind, we'd be practicing our balance and comedy at the same time.

Think of *The Karate Kid*. Remember the scene on the beach where Daniel sees Mr. Miyagi on a wooden bollard doing his crane-technique kicks, then later replicates them on a bollard of his own? Okay. Now imagine if Daniel saw Mr. Miyagi standing on a pillar, on one leg, doing stand-up comedy. Daniel would have realized Mr. Miyagi was an idiot.

So we had our crowd, our stage, and our sound system. But we forgot one thing. Who would go first? Everything was ready to go. Except us. We looked at one another, knowing the question before Mark actually asked it: "What's the order?"

The order? The nerve of this guy. It was obvious now that we were here in the cold and wind, and with a neck-breaking stage, that this idea had little chance of succeeding. It would be a miracle if any of us had the nerve to get up on that pylon and attempt some jokes, let alone have an order.

Still, we each played along so that we could goad someone into going first. We knew that in all likelihood that person would also be last, but we all bluffed to see which of us would go first. You know that kid's game when two people say something at the same time, and one says "Jinx" the other can't talk? Well, all three of us said at the same time, "I don't wanna go first."

I wish some outside third party had yelled, "Jinx!" so none of us could talk. That way we could go home in silence and forget the whole bad idea.

Instead we just stared at each other, shifting from one foot to the other, shivering but not from the cold. Comedy is tough under the best circumstances. You are getting up in front of total strangers and telling them you think you are funny. Speaking in public is the number one fear people have—just plain speaking. That's without the added pressure of having to get laughs.

Now, three stooges were going to attempt this incredibly difficult skill under ridiculous conditions. A seasoned professional comic would fail 99 times out of a 100 in this position. But we novices were going to try it.

I had something those seasoned professionals didn't: naïveté. I was young, dumb, and susceptible to peer pressure. After a long silence, one of the guys looked at me and said, "It was your idea."

The line had been drawn. This was my baby. I remained silent. I was more nervous than I'd ever been. My knees were wobbling as I looked at the crowd. I thought to myself, *I can't do this*. Finally Mark said, "Maybe this is a bad idea."

Yes! An out. It was a bad idea. We all agreed. I tried to mutter something about there being no way it could work, but my mouth was twitching from anxiety. Whatever came out didn't make sense. Drennon and Mark still got the idea that I didn't want to do it. They didn't want to, either. Finally we all nodded and Drennon went to unplug the amp from the Churro station.

Mark was a good friend of mine already. He was smart and funny. I respected him. He slapped me on the chest with the back of his hand, "It seemed like a good idea."

I looked at the line of people, each one staring into the back of the person in front of them. No one in line was talking to anyone else. Drennon walked back up with the extension cord. My mouth still wasn't working right, but I said, "Plug it back in, Drennon."

Drennon looked surprised. "You gonna do it?"

I gulped and nodded. To me the only thing worse than failure is regret. There was only one way to be sure this was a bad idea. Do it. Drennon plugged the amp back in. When he got back to the bollard, we exchanged glances. Drennon gave me a goofy smile that made me smile a bit. I grabbed the mic and took a deep breath. I put one hand on the bollard to get ready to step up. Mark looked me in the eye and said, "You've got the biggest set of balls I've ever seen."

After a comment like that there was no turning back. So on the heels of it, I threw my leg up and stepped onto the tiny cement stage. No one in the line noticed me yet. I licked my lips to force moisture into my mouth. It didn't help, but I lifted the mic to my mouth and said, "Hello, Everyone! Welcome to the Alcatraz Boat Line Comedy Show."

Almost everyone in the line turned toward me. Great! Maybe this could work? Nope. I attempted about three minutes of the very limited material I had and it got nothing. Maybe a groan here or there. Or maybe a smile from a mother who was trying to be nice because her teenage sons were mumbling that I sucked. By the end of the three minutes, half the audience wasn't listening anymore. They were happier waiting to go to jail than listening to me.

I decided to wrap it up and give one of the other guys a chance. I looked down at the guys. Drennon shook his head as if to say, "No way." Mark gave me a shrug that indicated, "What the hell."

"That's my time, lady and gentleman tourists! But I have another great comic here. Please welcome Mark Nadeau!"

Mark and I awkwardly switched places on the concrete pole. He did a couple of minutes and had about the same response and retention rate. When he ended by saying, "Thank you, and enjoy your visit," there was no applause, just a return to waiting and pretending like nothing had happened in the last ten minutes.

Mark got down. I patted him on the back.

"Let's get out of here," he said.

We quickly packed up and went somewhere warm. I don't remember where. It must be post-traumatic stress disorder. We talked about how bad it was, and Mark reiterated his "balls" compliment at some point. I tried to return the compliment for his efforts, but he shrugged it off. "I wouldn't have gone first."

I told him if I had to do it over again, neither would I.

After a while we laughed about it a bit, but not too much. The sting of the failure was too close . . . and too big. Eventually we left whatever warm place we were in. We never tried anything like that again. We just stuck to the traditional stage time. Sometimes now, after I have a great set, I wonder if with better material and a decade of experience under my belt, I could get that crowd? Then I shudder and try to forget it.

6

Impressing Robin Williams

At one of those open mics I went to every week, I met a comic named Lee Levine, who to this day remains one of my best friends. He is like a funny Moby, bald with glasses. We were both doing a sign-up show somewhere at a bar in Marin County, about twenty miles north of San Francisco. More comics were in the bar than were patrons. And there were only eight comics.

Lee had a really great set, with a lot of jokes about his temp job. Lee has a distinct way of talking. He grew up in Marin around a lot of hippies and says "groovy" a lot. One of the funniest things he does, which we all love imitating, is beginning many of his sentences with the word *yeah*. And he draws it out really long, as in, "Yeeeeaaaah, that was a pretty good set you had."

At that same show, I met a future roommate, a comic named John "Hoogie" Hoogasian. He was peculiar, awkward, and hilarious. I truly had never seen (and still haven't) another comic like him.

After the show, Lee came up and talked to me a bit. I asked him for advice on places to get stage time. He told me I should ask Hoogie, then introduced me to John. John was just as off-kilter offstage, but both he and Lee were really helpful. They were the first comics who weren't new like me, and were nice. They'd been doing comedy only a year or so longer than me, but so many comics ahead of me seemed unfriendly. Whenever I hung out at the comedy clubs, which was expected if you wanted stage time, the senior guys were off-putting. It was almost like some sort of hazing or pecking-order mentality. Ignore and be mean to the new guys. Why? Because that's what the senior guys did to them when they started.

I had seen this kind of frat behavior in the Navy, and it was one of the things I didn't like about the service. Many people have the attitude of "You've got to earn my respect." I thought that was stupid. I'm a human being. Who the hell are you to expect me to prove anything to you? My attitude is "You've got to earn my disrespect." I think the world would be better with more of that attitude.

I guess I've always gravitated toward people who have that approach, who don't have any pretense, and you feel like you can be yourself with them pretty quickly. I've been blessed with incredible friends my whole life, so my philosophy seems to be working out. Lee and John were those kinds of guys.

Months later I was at a bar in San Francisco called Ireland's 32. It was an open mic, but it was on Geary, a busy street, so it often had nice crowds. You could show up and sign up. But because it was getting such good buzz on the comedy scene, a lot of the veteran comics who didn't usually do open mics started showing up. Sometimes even famous, big-name comics dropped by.

Often when these more senior comics came in, the new guys would get bumped from the show, even though they signed up early. If you got bumped, your trip was wasted. But the guy who ran the show, Gary Cannon, would usually make it up to you by putting you up the following week and in a great spot.

When I first started hanging out at the comedy clubs, I thought Gary was the biggest comic in the city. I saw him two times in a row on the Sunday showcases of local talent at The Punch Line comedy club. He destroyed the crowd both times. He had one of the two best sets of the night both times I saw him. It turned out that Gary was only a couple of years ahead of me and the more I saw him perform the more I saw how inconsistent he was. He'd either have a great set or an awful one. But it was obvious to me and everyone else that he was onto something very funny.

Anyway, I was at Ireland's 32, getting what should have been a prime spot because Gary had bumped me the week before. Seven days earlier the bar had been packed and everyone who got up had a great set. I had been chomping at the bit to go up, but several of the big comics on the scene, like Arj Barker and Jim Short, showed up. Gary asked if he could bump me. (He asked, but really he was just nicely telling me.)

So here I was a week later. And no spot was prime. The bar was basically empty. Two people were there, and they were watching a game on TV. There were half a dozen comics, including Lee Levine, Gary, and another guy they hung out with named Chris Duffy. Chris was performing while the other comics were scattered around the room getting ready for their sets.

Finally, Gary came up and said I was next. He brought me up, and I started going into my act. I was maybe six months into comedy at this point. If I had any feedback from other comics, it was that I was too scripted, too stiff. I had good jokes but it always felt like I was telling jokes, not really there with the audience. Tonight that didn't matter too much because there was no audience.

But thirty seconds into my set, the couple at the bar who had watched Chris, turned their backs on me. So at this point all I saw was their backs, and about five comics with their heads down in their notebooks. I was delivering my script to no one. I saw Gary and Lee talking to each other way in the back. From the stage I could also see the front door. A minute into my monologue, Robin Williams walked in. He stood in the doorway and looked around. I was the only one who saw him. I told myself, *Robin Williams is watching you perform! Put it in another gear, Steve.*

The problem was, I didn't have another gear. I was maxing out already.

Robin saw me dying and playing to no one. He turned and walked out. I was crushed. I thought about yelling into the mic, "I sat through *Bicentennial Man!*" But truthfully I didn't think of that till the ride home. It didn't matter; I would have left, too.

I started to crack. It was all adding up. The awful set I was having, reciting lines to no one. The frustration of knowing how good the show had been on the night I got bumped. The long drives. The late nights and early mornings. And now Robin Williams walking out on me. I stopped doing my act. I just looked around. I wanted to cry. Was this what I had dreamed about all those years? This? All to feel this awful rejection? Maybe I should reconsider this comedy thing.

I just started rambling. "I think I'm not gonna do my whole five minutes. It just seems a little pointless to tell myself jokes that I've heard before. I know 'em. Hell, I wrote them."

Gary noticed I was off. We didn't know each other well at this point, but it would have been obvious to anyone listening that I was frustrated. But he was the only one listening. Or, at least, half-listening. Gary stopped talking to Lee and watched me for a second.

Then Gary did something amazing. He waved Lee to follow him. They called Chris over. All three of them came right in front of the stage and pulled up chairs. They looked up and paid attention. I appreciated what they were doing, but I was still frustrated. "You guys don't have to do that, I'm just gonna get off early."

Lee and Chris shook their heads. Gary said, "This is why you're here. To do your act for people. So do your time."

I went back into my act. The three of them laughed, even though they had already heard every joke I did.

What Lee, Gary, and Chris did that night was show me a real piece of humanity in a place where there usually isn't any. Comedy is competitive. Comedians are cynical. The actions of these three guys showed me that they had been through the same situations and they understood it wasn't easy. And they weren't going to let me give up. I finished and got off. Gary made the people at the bar and the other comics applaud for me. Had those guys not done what they did that night, I might have quit comedy. It's easily the closest I ever came to giving up.

7

Out of the Nest

The Punch Line and Cobb's Comedy Club were the two comedy clubs in San Francisco when I started. Punch Line was located on the roof of The Embarcadero Center, a shopping district near downtown. The first time I stepped foot inside Punch Line, I thought it was gigantic. With its wide-open showroom, it was certainly bigger than the tiny comedy clubs I had been to when I was in the Navy and college. The room was a large rectangle with a stage on one of the long sides and a bar on the opposite side. In between were hundreds of wooden chairs with green cushions arranged around dozens of tiny tables. On both short ends of the rectangle were raised wings, a few feet higher than the floor, where a few tables and booths stood. When I started, before the fire marshal pulled a bunch of seats, the club sat about 250 people.

The stage was a ten by twenty rectangle and featured a backdrop of a cartoony mural of San Francisco. It's funny how many goofy backgrounds comedy clubs have. The ceiling at Punch Line was super low. In fact if you were onstage, you could reach up and touch the overhead. Over the years I came to realize that comedy does not go as well in rooms with high ceilings. I guess the jokes get caught in the rafters somehow.

Cobb's Comedy Club had low ceilings, too, but was different in many ways. Located in The Cannery, which is right near Fisherman's Wharf, Cobb's was attached to a Cajun restaurant and was a much smaller club. When they really packed a crowd in there like a Japanese train, it sat around 175 or so. The building was square and relatively plain with bare walls, except for another goofy backdrop behind the small square stage. This backdrop was cartoony, as well, and depicted a living room with a table and lounge chair with a cat on it. It looked like you were performing in the Simpson's living room. The bar was removed from the showroom, down a small hallway. There were no distractions whatsoever. Even when only a quarter of the way filled, it felt full. The crowds could be explosive in that room.

Punch Line is located in an area that nobody goes to after work. So it really is a destination club. They book great comics and locals drive in from all over the Bay for shows. Cobb's vicinity to the wharf and lots of hotels resulted in crowds made up of tourists.

The dichotomy of the clubs and their audiences was great for comedians. San Franciscans are by nature liberal and tolerant. They are willing to laugh at anything. Nothing is off limits. But they want it to be smart and never cheap. This was the crowd Punch Line pulled in. Because Cobb's pulled in tourists, their crowds were the complete opposite of Punch Line's. They were generally more conservative, picky, and likely to be offended. Comics who performed at both clubs got a chance to play for a wide variety of audiences, and the experience made them really good.

The protocol for new comics at both clubs was basically the same. Hang out. Hang out long enough so that you didn't seem like a new face. Once you were recognized, the track at the clubs was a little different. At Punch Line you'd have to show up every Sunday night for the Comedy Showcase. Big name headliners would perform all week, Tuesday through Saturday, but Sunday was a show of a dozen local comedians. Because the scene had such a good reputation, this show would often have a big crowd even though it was late Sunday night. You never knew who was going to be on until about five minutes before the show started. Then the manager would walk around, see which comics were there, and start making a lineup. It was very stressful. You'd try to get noticed, but not try so hard that you came across as obnoxious. As many as fifty comics might be hanging out, and everyone wanted to be picked. It was like waiting to be picked for kickball teams in grade school. The first five comedians or so would be chosen right before the show, and the other ten or so after the show started.

The girl who ran the Punch Line show when I started wasn't very nice. She's no longer there, and I'm not sure what she's doing now, but I pray it is not customer service. The senior comics told me the guy who managed before her was even worse. I couldn't imagine how, unless he physically beat comics. This girl was the saddest person I had ever met. I never saw her smile in two years. I'll kindly refer to her as Manager Sad Sack.

Manager Sad Sack didn't seem to enjoy any part of comedy or comedians. Any time I saw her talking to someone, it looked like she was being inconvenienced and wanted to end the conversation as quickly as possible. When she walked into the room each Sunday night, every comic tensed. All laughter hushed. She was like a mean school teacher everyone tiptoed around. I was new to stand-up, but I knew that this was a bad recipe for comedy.

Putting all the performers in a crappy, stressed mood couldn't bring out their best performances.

Anyway, after hanging out there between three to six months, Manager Sad Sack would eventually come up and say, "Do you wanna do a set?"

"Nah, I just like hanging out in this agitated cesspool week after week for nothing." I never said that. Of course, I, or whoever she asked that, wanted to do a set. No one would choose to be in that neurotic waiting room without a possible payoff.

So once you said yes, she told you what spot you were going up in. Then you had anywhere between ten and twenty minutes to get ready. When I got my first set, I walked outside to practice. Lee, Gary, Chris, and Mark slapped me on the back on the way out because they had seen me get chosen. They had all been up before and were rooting for me. I was so nervous. If the set went wrong, it would be several more months of hanging out before I was given another chance. I went around the corner from the entrance and ran through my set a couple times. Then I took a deep breath and went back inside. The guy on the list before me was on, so I waited in the wings.

I ended up having a pretty good set. Not great, but good for being so nervous and wanting to make a good impression. The important thing was it was good enough that I started getting sets on the Punch Line Sunday Showcase once a month or so.

Cobb's had the craziest system I've ever heard of for breaking into the club. Because of all the travelers in the area, they would have three showcases a week: Monday, Tuesday, and Wednesday. After hanging out at the club for a couple months, the owner, Tom Sawyer (yes, that's really his name), would say, "You can start calling in."

This meant that on those three days, you called in to the club precisely at 3:00 PM for a chance to be on the showcase that night. It was like a radio contest. Every comedian in the city was on the phone calling in for one of fifteen spots. The line was always busy. If you didn't get an answer by 3:04, you weren't on and might as well give up calling. And even if you got through, you weren't definitely on. Tom, or his assistants, Ben and Terry, would answer the phone and you'd say as fast as possible, "Steve Mazan calling in for a set?"

Then they'd say either, "See you tonight," or "Call back tomorrow."

Getting on was like winning a contest. You'd jump up and down and scream. If they said no, you felt like a loser until you could call the next day. The only thing worse than not getting on was getting a call from one of your friends saying he did get on.

"Hello?"

"Hey, is this Fresh Wound?"

"Yes."

"It's your old buddy, Salt! Guess what?"

Click.

Tom made the lineup for the show as he took calls. He organized the list by seniority. So there weren't really fifteen spots open to everyone. There were one or two spots of five minutes for new comics; two or three seven-minute spots for comics who had been doing it a little longer. Comics getting paid work at the club, about seven of those spots, got ten-minute sets. Then, the biggest local comics, headliners, would close the show with fifteen minutes. There were two or three of those spots. As you got better, you moved up the list.

I got my first showcase set at Punch Line, but I got up with a lot more regularity at Cobb's. For some reason Cobb's saw something in me and gave me a set or two a week. I only did one or two five-minute sets before graduating to the seven-minute section. I remember the day I arrived at Cobb's for my set and saw that I had moved beyond the "newbie" section. It's still one of my most thrilling times in comedy.

Cobb's also gave me my first paid week of work. One night after a particularly good seven-minute set, I walked out of the showroom into the restaurant. Tom called me over to the check-in stand. He asked me if I wanted to host a week the following month. Of course I did!

On my drive home that night I punched the roof of my car and let out another "woo-hoo!" As happy as I was, I felt weird about sharing the good news with Lee and Gary. They were both getting work at Punch Line, and had been doing comedy a lot longer than I had at that point. But they hadn't been given paid work at Cobb's yet. They both felt they should be getting work there. I had moved through the ranks pretty quickly and knew it could be a sore subject when I brought it up. This is obviously the problem with being such good friends with people you work with: as happy as you are when good things happen for them, there is also a little jealousy. Getting news that your friend got work at Cobb's was like hearing from your old buddy Salt *and* his friend Tabasco.

It took me much longer to get paid work at Punch Line. In fact it was almost a year later, when Manager Sad Sack left her job to spread her cheer elsewhere, that I got a hosting week there. Molly, the new manager, was friendly, approachable, and, best of all, really liked comedy. The mood at the club, especially among the comics, improved immediately. Comics started looking forward to hanging out the club rather than dreading it. A great new wave of young comics hit the scene around that time, and Molly was part of the reason.

Even after I was getting regular sets at the clubs, I still went to open mics. It was important to get up as much as possible. On Mondays I'd often do a showcase set at Cobb's and then drive an hour south to an English bar in Palo Alto called The Rose & Crown, not too far from the Stanford University campus. The Crown, as we called it, was why I became a good comic so quickly. Comedy night started there about a month after I began comedy, and I think I missed only four Mondays at The Crown in over three years.

The Rose & Crown's comedy night was successful right from the beginning. They always had a crowd. If there was any problem at the start, it was that there weren't enough comics at the show. Palo Alto lies almost directly between San Jose and San Francisco, about thirty miles from each city. So it was a little out of the way for comedians who lived in either of these cities and impossible to get to if you didn't have a car. Many comics didn't own a car. Owning my own car, my beloved Pontiac Grand Prix GTP, afforded me a lot of road work early on. Bookers could count on me, and other comics requested to work with me so I could give them a ride.

The location of The Rose & Crown kept a lot of comedians from showing up for its open mic during the first eight months or so that it was running. Several Mondays I showed up and only two or three other comics were there. But there was a full crowd waiting to see comedy. So I got to do as much time as I wanted. I was getting only five minutes at every other place I went, but at The Crown I could do fifteen or twenty. In the beginning I didn't even have that much material. So I would just tell as many of my jokes as I could, and then talk to the audience. I'd ask questions and try to be funny. I'd do that for as long as I could, and then I'd tell the one joke I had left in my pocket so that I'd leave on a sure laugh.

Lee Levine, Mark Nadeau, Hoogie, and I knew the value of stage time in front of a smart, college-age audience, so we showed up religiously. We even got upset when other comics started coming down because word had gotten out about how good the shows were. Newspapers ran articles on The Crown's first anniversary show, causing even more comics to show up. But I always felt like it was my home. I owe my style, my first hour of good material, and probably my career to The Crown.

The entire time I pursued comedy in San Francisco, I held down the same day job at Sterling Personnel. My bosses, Marilyn and Ute, were extremely supportive of my comedy career. There were so many start-ups throwing around money that most employees were hopping every month to better paying jobs. But I wasn't interested in moving to a new job for a bigger salary; I was interested in having a set schedule I could do comedy around. My bosses knew this and appreciated that I didn't leave for any of the lucrative positions that we were available. To reward me, they were flexible. They'd give me time off to go on the road and do comedy shows in other states, even when I didn't have vacation days. And they continued paying me. Their support helped me to capitalize on every comedy opportunity that came my way.

Sterling Personnel had numerous phones with multiple lines at our office. At 3:00 PM on Cobb's showcase days, Marilyn, Ute, Bianca, our receptionist, my coworker Dave, and I would all dial in to get me on the show. We'd all keep calling in and hanging up on busy signals until one of us got a ring. Then they'd switch the line to me before it got picked up. One time Ute waited until Cobb's answered, and said, "This is Steve Mazan's boss calling in to get him a set."

Surprisingly, Tom said, "Okay, we'll see him tonight."

Ute was so proud. She was giddy that she had gotten me on the show that day. It's one of my favorite memories of her. Sadly, Ute died of cancer after a long fight while I was still working at Sterling. Marilyn ran the company alone after that.

Looking back now, I realize the value of having that job when I started comedy. It allowed me to live in an expensive city and pay for a car and gas for all the driving I did to faraway gigs. I know several comics who fell out of the business because their jobs they couldn't afford to lose interfered with comedy.

Unfortunately—but ultimately, fortunately—the dot-com bubble burst. By 2002 the economy and the jobs in the Bay Area dried up. The start-ups were gone. No one was hiring, so Sterling was struggling. Marilyn kept me on longer than she should have. It became obvious that she needed to cut Sterling's staff, and someone would be let go. Still, I had it good and didn't want to be fired.

Marilyn called me into her office one slow day and said she had to decrease the staff. "You're one of my best employees, but I know your heart is in comedy. The other employees need a day job. I'm pushing you out of the nest so that you'll commit to stand-up full time."

I appreciated her saying it, but I was still incredibly scared. I knew hundreds of comedians, but I knew only a few who did it full time. It was tough to make a living at it. I don't know if I ever would have made the choice to try it as a full-time career on my own. Now, I had no choice.

8

L.A. Woman

The minute I was out of a day job, I started contacting every comedy club I had played and asked for work. Most of the ones I hadn't performed at in the last few months gave me a week. I felt better when I had a bunch of work on my calendar. When I wasn't working, I hit open mics and wrote as much as possible.

When I first moved to the Bay Area, I lived close to the office, out in the East Bay in the suburb of Fremont. But by the time I was let go from Sterling, I had been living in San Francisco for over a year. It was a much longer commute to work, but more convenient at night when I was doing comedy. The apartment I lived in was pretty famous in the SF comedy scene.

I lived at 336 21st Avenue, but it was referred to as "The Comedy Condo." Usually that term refers to an apartment a comedy club rents out and puts up visiting comedians, rather than renting multiple hotel rooms each week. But in this case, it was an apartment that only comedians had lived in for over fifteen years. It had no ties to any of the clubs, just the comics on the scene.

Sometime in 1986, two comics, Dana Gould and Alex Reid, rented the place. Years after moving out of "The 336," Dana became a writer for *The Simpsons* and Alex became a producer on *Malcolm in the Middle*. Somehow a tradition started that only comics could move into the house. So if you lived there and wanted to move out, you had to find a comic to take your place.

I moved in when a hilarious impressionist named Colin Mahan decided to move to Los Angeles. Hoogie was already living there at the time, and Mark Nadeau, whom I performed with at Fisherman's Wharf, took the third bedroom soon after I moved in.

As storied as the place was, it was also a piece of crap: dark, dingy, and damp. I lived on the second floor of the building, but it felt like a basement. That area of the city is known as the Outer Richmond, and is famous for its lack of sunshine. If you've seen photos of the fog in San Francisco, this is where it is manufactured. Hanging up a towel to dry was a futile act. Mark and I immediately went to Home Depot and bought some paint and lamps to brighten up the place. It helped. A little. At least now people felt like coming over and hanging out. So many comedians performing in the area crashed on our couch during the time I was there that I can't remember all of them.

One day while cleaning the place, Mark and I found a book that listed all the comedians who had ever lived, crashed, or just partied there. The list included Janeane Garafolo, Margaret Cho, David Cross, Louis C.K., and *The Daily Show* creator, Lizz Winstead. It was a pretty impressive group. I'm sure many more passed through the house who never made the book because we hadn't even known about it. Who knew when it had last been updated?

In the months after losing my day job, I'd sleep in, write material, try to book work, and then go out to the shows at night. That's if I wasn't working at a club out of town. Evenutally I started feeling like I had stopped moving forward. I was now hosting weeks at both Punch Line and Cobb's and was featuring (the next step up) at The Improv, which had recently opened in San Jose.

I was ready to feature at every club in the area, but so many comics were ahead of me that it was hard to move up. Usually comics would work their way up to the feature spot, which was thirty minutes of stage time, hang out for a year or two to get really good, and then move to Los Angeles or New York. But no one ahead of me on the scene was moving. It was a comedy logjam. And I was at the back of it.

I came to understand a couple of reasons why. First, San Francisco is an unbelievable city. World class. New York and Los Angeles are great places, but when the weather is good in San Francisco, there is no better place on the planet. It's amazing—picturesque, full of landmarks and things to do, and it offers great food and great art. And all of it in a very tiny area compared to the big cities. So it's a hard place to leave. If you can choose to live anywhere, this is as good as it gets.

As great a city as it is, it's also an amazing place for comedy. As I mentioned, the number of clubs and shows with a wide array of audiences offers a rare chance to become a great comic without having to travel too much. And the scene took comedy seriously, so you felt like an artist, not just an entertainer. Moving anywhere else would be a step down as far as how the craft was treated.

Most of all though, comics didn't move because they were scared. New York and Los Angeles were where you moved to be discovered. There were thousands of comedians in those places, not hundreds. If you were funny in San Francisco, eventually someone would notice and you could work your way up the clubs.

But in New York and L.A., you could get lost. I saw several great comics move away and return within a year or two because they couldn't get noticed.

Plus, starting comedy is one of the hardest things to do. So if you have started and made a name for yourself, why would you leave just to start all over again in a new place? Why repeat that awful beginning? None of this made it easy to move away. But for some reason, in 2003 there was an extra-big bottleneck of comedians who hadn't moved on. And it was affecting me. The conventional wisdom on the scene was never to move to L.A. or New York before you started consistently featuring at all the clubs in those areas. With the back-up of comics at the top, it might take me two or three more years to make that happen.

By then I was thirty-two, and because I didn't start stand-up until I was twenty-nine, I already felt old. Most comedians start in their early twenties. When agents came to town to look at San Francisco talent, they always focused on the young guys. I guess because they have more time to cultivate that talent. This always seemed shortsighted to me, because every huge sitcom star ended up being a comic who was in their late thirties or forties (Seinfeld, Roseanne, Ray Romano . . .). In any case, it seemed like youth was valued just as much as talent. And I definitely wasn't getting younger. If I waited until featuring spots opened up, I might not move until I was thirty-five or thirty-six. I looked young, but that age wouldn't impress anyone if I was just arriving in Los Angeles.

It became obvious that I would have to ignore the usual path and leave while I was just a host. To be clear, I was already featuring at every club outside of San Francisco, and even headlining at a couple. For some reason, in comedy, you always move up slowest in your home city. I call it "the puppy syndrome," where your home clubs are too close and see you so often they don't notice the growth.

So I chose to leave. Now I had to decide between moving to Los Angeles or New York. My age would not be as big a factor in New York. New York was more concerned with funny than age. That scene was about comedy—about growing great stand-ups. Los Angeles was more about finding stand-ups who were young, good looking, and could be used for TV projects and movies. Funny mattered, but not as much.

I didn't care about TV or movies. I cared about stand-up. I wanted to get as good as I could. I wouldn't turn down TV or movies, but they would only be to make me more known as a comedian. TV and movies weren't the ultimate goal. Stand-up was. That outlook pointed with every arrow to New York City. But I chose L.A.

Los Angeles had something important that NYC did not— year-round warm weather. More than two decades of living in Chicago-land left me hating cold weather. Somewhere in my late twenties I told myself that I would never pick up a snow shovel again. I would never scrape ice off my windshield again. Los Angeles fit that plan.

As a bonus, I also had a few friends down there. Gary Cannon had left San Francisco a year earlier for the same reasons and was now living in Santa Monica. Lee Levine had moved to Los Angeles about six months after Gary and was sharing a room with a comic named Robert Duchaine. Robert was a veteran comic who had spent a couple years in San Francisco, too.

My friends and the friendly weather made Los Angeles the easy choice. If I was basically going to be starting over in a new comedy scene, I might as well do it with some close friends. We could share the rough patches together and hopefully make them easier.

Once I made my decision, I told my roommates, John and Mark, and the other comics on the scene. One of the funny young comics named Ryan Stout ended up taking my place at The Comedy Condo. Sadly, The 336 apartment lasted only another two years before the landlord kicked everyone out to do renovations, and raised the rent to an amount comics could never afford. A comedy institution had come to an end, but luckily I had been a part of it.

When I told everyone I was leaving, a comic named Sean Robinson told me he was thinking of moving, too. Sean had moved to San Francisco from Vancouver, and we had recently started hanging out a bunch. Canadians tend to be super funny, and Sean was no exception. He had a day job that he could transfer to Southern California. We decided we'd move down together.

Lee Levine and Robert Duchaine were sharing a studio apartment in the Sherman Oaks area of L.A. at the time. Robert slept in the walk-in closet when they were both in town. When they heard Sean and I were moving down, they suggested we all get a place together. We could save on rent by having four roommates. And maybe we'd be starting a "Comedy Condo" tradition in L.A.

Lee and I found a three-bedroom apartment in North Hollywood. The place was pretty nice, especially compared to my dingy, dark place in San Francisco. Best of all, it was cheap. The problem was it had only three bedrooms, but we had four people. Robert and I decided to share one room. Heck, he had been sleeping in a closet, so this was a step up. Plus, Robert and I were both gone a lot, working clubs on the road. Very few times would we both be in Los Angeles.

I was in my thirties and sharing a room with another grown man. Yet I was as happy as I'd ever been.

It was hard starting in a new scene. But I wasn't doing it alone. Lee and Gary introduced me to a lot of their friends and the comedy rooms they were doing. We started hanging out at the Hollywood Improv as much as possible. I saw a lot of great comics. It was exciting and intimidating at the same time.

The weather was fantastic. You could go out every single day. If there was ever a problem, it was that it was too hot. Being the entertainment capital of the world and having beautiful weather also ensured that there was no shortage of beautiful and scantily dressed women. So although it wasn't easy being new on the scene, there were plenty of things to make it worthwhile.

My first couple of years in Los Angeles I learned about another comedy catch-22. To be discovered in comedy you need to be in L.A., but to make any money at comedy you had to go on the road. There were so many comics in L.A. that the clubs didn't pay. So I'd spend a lot of time on the road playing clubs in Illinois, Indiana, Wisconsin, Nevada, Idaho, Texas, Arizona, New Mexico, Colorado, and everywhere else across the country.

If the club I was booked at was within seven hours, I'd drive. If it was farther, I'd fly. I love driving. Some people would never choose to drive that far, but I find it therapeutic. There is nothing like driving across a state for hours at a time with nothing but the radio and your thoughts. I always loved throwing my bags into the trunk of my Pontiac and hitting the road for a long trip. I'd practice my set over and over. I'd come up with new jokes and listen to CDs of my favorite comedians like Mitch Hedberg, Brian Regan, and Bill Hicks. Some people would find it lonely, but I looked forward to it each time I went on the road.

I spent my time "in town" in Los Angeles trying to be seen at the clubs or comedy rooms and hanging out with my comic friends. During the day I'd write and try to get work at new clubs I hadn't been to. I had to send clubs a VHS tape of my stand-up for them to review and decide if they wanted to give me work. Slowly the industry was changing to DVDs. We had a few VCRs at our place to copy tapes, but nothing to mass copy and edit DVDs. So I started asking around about where I could get some comedy DVDs edited from my comedy tapes.

Gary was dating Sue Nelson, a comic. Sue knew a married couple who lived in her building and edited actors' reels. She was positive they could do a good job with stand-up comedy, too. Sue gave me their names: Joke and Biagio.

"What?"

Sue repeated, "Joke, as in tell a joke, and Biagio."

I was confused. Which one was the wife and which was the husband? No one where I grew up had either of these names. How had these two people found each other? I called the number and talked to Joke, the wife. She said that Biagio could definitely edit my comedy tapes and put them on a DVD. We set up a time to meet at their place.

Joke was from Belgium, where her name is not uncommon. Biagio's name was Italian, but he grew up in Ohio. They worked out of their one-bedroom apartment. Their editing equipment took up most of their living room. I liked both of them right away. The best way to describe them was that they seemed real. There is definitely a "fake" vibe you get from a lot of people in Hollywood, but there was no trace of it from either of them. They were both complimentary about my comedy, but it didn't feel like they were just saying it because I was paying them. They were sincere. They felt like people I'd like to hang out with.

Biagio loaded up all my tapes and started picking out the best parts. I directed him a little bit, but he had a great eye on how things should best be strung together. If we disagreed about which of two jokes should be used, Joke would be the deciding vote. For the most part, Joke worked on the phone or did other projects. But a couple times when Biagio was busy making an edit super smooth, Joke and I would make small talk. Joke told me they were aspiring filmmakers and TV producers who had met while they were at UCLA.

I asked what they had done so far.

"We've done a documentary about *Star Wars* fans, and another film we both produced and directed."

In less than an hour Biagio had taken a dozen different sets of mine and made an impressive highlight package of my comedy. They told me to let them know when I was performing in town. I left incredibly satisfied. I knew I'd get a lot of work from these DVDs, and I'd made a couple new friends.

That DVD did get me into a lot of new clubs. I was on the road more and more. Lee and Robert were on the road as much as I was. Sean had settled into his day job but was still going out at night and on the weekends for stage time. Gary never left Los Angeles but was making more of a dent in the industry than the rest of us.

When he left the Bay Area, Gary was not getting much respect from the clubs. He was hosting at Punch Line and had never gotten paid work at Cobb's. But something happened when he moved to Southern California. I don't know if it was a confidence thing or what, but Gary started impressing everyone who saw him. He had always been funny, but now he was consistently funny. He had reached a new level.

As a result, Gary got regular sets at The Improv, and had even started doing audience warm-up for a number of television shows. Eventually he landed a permanent position doing audience warm-up for *The Carson Daly Show*.

Although the L.A. clubs didn't pay for sets, the Improv had three clubs out in the suburbs that did pay. At some point in the summer of 2004, Gary picked up a Tuesday night at the Ontario, California, Improv to headline a show. As funny as Gary is, he doesn't write a lot of jokes. Even though he had been doing comedy for five years, he didn't have more than fifteen minutes of material. That wasn't enough to headline. So Gary called the show "Gary Cannon & Friends" and invited a bunch of his friends to take part.

I was in town that week, so Gary invited me down and asked if I'd host the show. I said sure. He had a couple other comics doing short sets after me, and then he would do fifteen or so minutes. After him, Kenny Kane, another Bay Area comic who had moved down, was headlining the show. Kenny was high-energy and wild and would be perfect to close the show.

Kenny, a good-looking, super-fit, incredibly positive, nice guy, attracted good-looking women. Kenny brought his new girlfriend, Ally, a yoga instructor, to the show. She sat up front with her mother.

The show started, and I took the stage as the host. Hosting is the hardest spot on a comedy show. The host has to take a cold audience and get it hot for the other comics. They take the crowd from zero to laughing in ten or fifteen minutes. Hopefully. Though the host controls the direction of the show, audiences often discount the talent of a host. As funny as any host is, they'd be even funnier if they weren't starting the show.

I took pride in being a good host. A comic I looked up to when I started, Larry "Bubbles" Brown, told me "Great hosts make great headliners." So I always worked hard at being a good host. That night I had the crowd right away. I was having a set that was good enough to be in the middle of the show. It felt great.

About five minutes into my set, a great-looking woman came in and sat with Kenny's girlfriend, Ally. I found her sexy. I was almost distracted by her, but I didn't want to start bombing in front of her, so I forced myself to focus and keep getting big laughs. It worked. I had a great set and left the stage to a big round of applause.

Each time I took the stage to introduce the next comic, I would try to get a good look at the girl with Ally. I wanted to stare at her but that wouldn't make a good impression. She looked good, and I thought I saw her smiling at me once.

Before Kenny went up, I asked, "Who's the girl sitting with Ally?"

"Oh, that's her friend, Denise."

After Kenny finished his set, I took the stage to thank everyone for coming out, and I made eye contact with Denise. I told myself to get off the stage and meet her. I must have stared too long because when I got off the stage and approached the table, Denise was quickly heading toward the exit. I was determined to meet her, so I started working my way through the crowd after her. Unfortunately, Ally's mother moved in front of me and introduced herself. When I looked up, Denise was gone.

A few days later Kenny called me. "Hey, remember that girl with Ally, Denise?"

"Of course."

"She asked Ally and me about you a couple of times times. You interested?"

"Very."

Kenny gave me her number and suggested I give her a call.

This was perfect. I had been thinking about her since I saw her, and it turns out she was thinking about me, too. Maybe she wasn't running. I normally would have been nervous calling a girl I had never met, but I felt like we had already shared a moment. Plus, she was interested, so I was very confident when she answered my call.

"Hi, Denise?"

"Yes."

"This is Steve, Kenny's friend from the comedy show the other night."

"Oh, the host?"

"Yeah, the host."

"You were really funny for the host."

"Huh?"

"Well usually the hosts aren't funny, even when they are comics."

"What? What do you mean if they're comics?"

"Well, you know, a lot of times they aren't really comics, just some guy who works at the club and makes announcements."

"Uh. No. That never happens. All the hosts are real comics."

"Oh, really?"

"Yeah, really."

"I didn't know that. That's why I didn't feel bad coming in late, because I figured you weren't really a comic. But then you ended up being really funny."

Wow. We were off to a terrible start, based on her knowledge and respect of comedy. But how could I hold her ignorance against her? I probably didn't know a lot about her job. Plus, she thought I was funny, so that went a long way toward letting it slide.

We ended up talking for just a couple minutes. She was actually out shopping and couldn't talk very long. She was cute even on the phone. We wrapped up the call but made a date for that weekend. I was ecstatic.

I was heading out for a long road trip the following Monday, so it was great to be able to schedule something before I left. If Denise and I couldn't do something that weekend, it would be three weeks till we could go on a date. It turned out that Denise, Kenny, and Ally were all going to an engagement party already, so I tagged along. Like a group date.

We all met at Ally's house on Saturday night. I was nervous because I still hadn't met Denise face-to-face. Kenny met me at the door and invited me in. As I was talking to Ally, Denise strode in from the kitchen. She wore high heels, tight jeans, and an off-the-shoulder blouse. A sexy outfit. Her reddish brown hair was curly and big. Going through puberty in the '80s had left me with a fondness for big hair. But the thing I remember most was her eyes—brighter and bluer than I'd remembered.

We went out to a nice restaurant with about six of their other friends. The food was great and so was the company. Denise was easy to talk to, and we had some private conversations as the night went on.

Denise worked two jobs. She was a yoga instructor and also ran youth and seniors programs at the YMCA in Pacific Palisades. She was the youngest of her siblings, like me, and had lived in San Francisco when I had. Her parents were divorced, too. Denise had grown up in the small northern California town of Ukiah. I had performed comedy a few times in Ukiah, but never while she lived there.

After dinner, Denise suggested we go to another party her

friend was throwing. Kenny and Ally didn't want to go, so I hopped into Denise's Kermit-green VW bug and off we went. Her friend Heidi lived pretty close by, but it was nice to have a little alone time with Denise on the drive. Because she was driving and no one else was around, I was able to stare at her a little longer than was probably appropriate. She was very attractive.

We had fun at the party, but didn't stay too long. Denise admitted to me weeks later that she just took me there so her close friends could get a look at me and see if I passed muster. I'm glad I didn't know then that I was going through the human equivalent of The Westminster Dog Show. "Hmmm, nice posture. Does what he's told. Went to bathroom in right place. Not bad. Maybe not Best in Show, but possibly Best in Breed."

Denise drove me back to my car at Ally's. On the way I told her I had a great time, and that I hoped we could get together, just her and me. She seemed open to it. When she dropped me off I leaned over and kissed her good-night.

Before I got into my car, I leaned through her car window. She told me to call her about scheduling a date after my road trip. Yes! She must like me. I hopped into my car and drove home on the 405. I didn't get far before I realized I didn't want to wait a whole three weeks before seeing her again. I know about the three-day rule, but I couldn't help myself. I called her on my drive home.

"Hello?"

"Hi, it's Steve."

"Wow, when I said to call, I didn't mean in five minutes."

I laughed. I hoped she wouldn't pick up on my nervousness. "I didn't want to wait till I got back, so is there any way we could meet tomorrow?"

"I have plans . . . in the evening."

"Well, then, how about lunch and maybe a movie?"

"Okay, see you tomorrow."

I love Mexican food, and to my delight, so does Denise. So the next day we went to her favorite Mexican restaurant. She ordered the fresh guacamole, which they make right at the table. Then we went to see the Vince Vaughn–Ben Stiller movie *Dodgeball*.

I walked up to one of those automatic ticket kiosks to buy the tickets. Denise came up and hugged me from behind while she looked over my shoulder. I don't know how I managed to buy the right tickets. She felt so great. It was sexy and tender at the same time. I liked that she could be affectionate.

The movie was great, but not as good as the date. After the movie I went back to Denise's place and met her roommate, Deva. Then Denise showed me her room and introduced me to her two dachshunds, Cali and Lexie. One was brown and one was black. Then Denise said, "My plans tonight are with Deva and some other friends. They'll be here soon, so I have to start getting ready."

I was about to leave when she grabbed me and started kissing me. I wasn't going to put a stop to it, but eventually she said, "Okay, you really gotta go now." I kissed her good-bye and left. I called her again on the way home.

"So, do you always do this?" Denise teased.

"No. This is definitely something new. I must really like you." I felt brave admitting that. Our phones became a really big part of our relationship early on.

Denise and I ended up talking on the phone at least once a day for my entire three-week road trip. Before or after every show I did, we talked, sometimes for over an hour. It was a great way to get to know each other. We talked about everything—childhood, adulthood, childhood dreams, adult dreams. Everything.

Three months later we were in love and seeing each other every day that I was in town. One time we went on a double date with one of her friends, who inevitably asked, "How did you guys meet?"

I recounted the story about seeing her at a comedy show and thinking I had missed my chance. But then Kenny called me and said that Denise had been asking Ally about me and—

Denise grabbed my arm and looked me in the eye. "I never asked about you."

"What?"

"I never asked about you. I didn't want to meet you. Ally and Kenny kept pestering me over and over. I kept saying no, but finally told them they could give you my number if they'd just leave me alone. Then when you called and we talked, I kind of became interested. But I never asked about you."

I was shocked. The whole basis of what I thought was our initial attraction was wrong. Then it hit me: If I hadn't thought she asked about me, I would never have been so confident when I called her. Thank God for big fat liars.

9

A Comedy of Errors

After about six months of dating, Denise, her two wiener dogs, and I moved in together into a small house that was divided into three apartments. Ours was a tiny one bedroom that also had a small cement backyard and a third of a garage that could be used as an office. The backyard was great for the dogs. We were happy.

I know we were happy because the first sixty days we lived together were two of the worst months of our lives. From the minute we moved in together, everything went to hell. But we made it through, loving each other even more.

Shortly after we were in the new place, one of Denise's dachshunds got sick. The black one, Lexie, started alternately convulsing and lying completely still and peeing blood. We rushed her to the after-hours vet. The doctor gave her some medicine and said he thought Lexie had eaten something really bad. She got better quickly. But Denise and I now had an unexpected $300 vet bill in a month we were already strapped from a paying a security deposit in addition to the first and last months' rent.

Later that week, Denise was laid off her job at the YMCA. I was so stressed. We had just moved into a place that I was afraid was too expensive, and now the person I was splitting the rent with didn't have a job. I started scrambling and booked crappy gigs I had told myself I'd never do again. But as long as it paid, I would do it.

Denise managed to get another job relatively quick. She's smart, and the economy was pretty good in 2005, so it wasn't too tough for someone like her to find something. Her new job was running an acting studio in Burbank. We were in Culver City, which is on the west side of Los Angeles, and Burbank is about twenty miles north. Twenty miles takes about an hour in Los Angeles traffic. It was a big commute, but not much tougher than the one she had to the YMCA, and at least she had a job.

The owner of the acting studio hired Denise to run the day-to-day business and to oversee the sales team. Denise was excited about the job because she had always wanted to own her own yoga and dance studio, and she thought this was a great opportunity to get paid to learn how to run a business. This job was one of the few good things that came along that month.

Denise worked long days at the new job, followed by a long commute. I worried about her driving home safely. Turns out I should have been worrying about myself. One dark and rainy night, I was coming home from a show in L.A. and had just turned onto our block. I got three houses from our place and an SUV ran a stop sign and hit my car. We were both going about thirty miles per hour when he slammed into the front right side of my car. The collision drove me and my Grand Prix up onto a neighbor's lawn. It happened so quickly that once my car came to a stop I finally realized what had occurred.

Uninjured but shaken, I got out of the car and walked up to the

SUV. A guy in his fifties got out of the driver's seat and a teenager out of the passenger side. We were all okay. Their vehicle was not too badly damaged and was driveable, so that was good.

What wasn't good was my car. My beautiful white Pontiac. It was wrecked. I was so sad. This was the first new car I had ever owned outright. I bought it when I had a great year at my day job in San Francisco. It had leather seats, a moonroof, and a great stereo system. I loved driving it. My friends called it The Whale, because it was big and white like Moby Dick. Comedy took me all across the country and this car had been with me on most of the trips. There were probably months I spent more time in that car than I did in my own apartment. It was like my pet. I was sad when the insurance company told me it was totaled.

Losing that car was an extra blow because I hadn't had a car payment for three years. That was about to change. Even with the other guy's insurance paying me a lump sum, it wasn't nearly enough to get a reliable car for road trips. In two weeks I had upped my rent and picked up a car payment; not great for someone who was always worried about money.

At the end of that month, I drove with Gary out to a show we were both on at the Ontario Improv. We took my new-to-me used car, a purple VW Golf. It was okay, but nowhere near as fun and comfy as my Whale. I don't remember how the show went that night. Gary and I have done so many together over the years a lot of them run together. One thing I know is that we were planning to grab a bite to eat on the way home.

Some comics can eat right before they go onstage, but not me. I'd rather go up hungry than have a lump in my stomach. But one reason why I love Gary is because he loves food as much as me. My weight fluctuates about twenty pounds and Gary yo-yos, too. Most of the increases come when we are hanging out a lot. We are bad influences on each other. Lee is the third point in this Bermuda Triangle of overeating.

Lee wasn't with us that night, but we were planning to eat some extra food in his honor. Gary and I had some mozzarella sticks at the club while the show was going but planned on getting something better on the way home.

Almost as soon as we left the club I started feeling bad. Ridiculously, I thought maybe it was because I hadn't eaten in a while and was hungry. I say ridiculously because I can't really think of any time in my life when I ate because I was hungry. Hunger is not a sensation I usually feel, because I eat mostly out of boredom or socially. It's hard to remember a time when my stomach growled because it needed food. One of the benefits of living in America, I guess.

Gary and I kept looking for exits that had restaurant signs but couldn't find any. By the time Gary saw a Denny's sign off in the distance, I knew my stomach wasn't hurting because it was empty. I told Gary there was no way I could go to Denny's. Five minutes later I told him I thought I had eaten something bad and I didn't think I could stop at all. Ten minutes later I was so uncomfortable, I pulled over and asked Gary to drive. The pain kept getting worse. I wasn't sure where it was coming from; all I knew was that it hurt. A lot. By the time we got to my place forty minutes later, I had crawled to the backseat and was moaning in pain.

Gary had called Denise on the drive and asked her if she thought we should go to the hospital. She said to bring me home and then she'd take me if I needed to go. Gary and Denise put me in bed. Denise was convinced I had food poisoning. I had never had it before, so I didn't know what it felt like.

After a couple of hours, the pain increased and became more intense with each passing minute. At some point I told Denise that we needed to go to the emergency room. She said it was just food poisoning and that I'd start throwing up, then it wouldn't be as intense. For the first time in my life, I looked forward to vomiting.

It may sound insensitive that Denise didn't take me to the hospital right away, but I understood. She didn't know how bad the pain was. Everything pointed to food poisoning. I had eaten something from a comedy club, which is not known for fine cuisine. Having never had food poisoning, I could only go with what people have told me about the symptoms. On top of that, we had just gone through an incredibly awful month financially, so the last thing we needed was to add an emergency room bill to the list, especially if it was something that would solve itself.

So I kept trying to fight the pain. Denise lay next to me the whole time, rubbing my back and whispering that it would be all right. She even tried to perform a Reiki healing on me—a spiritual therapy that Denise had studied. It's a Japanese technique of hands-on healing, involving touching and waving your hands over an injured area to get the "life force" flowing. The idea is that health problems come from blocks on this "life force," and if you can return flow, everything will be better. When I was growing up, I never heard any doctor in Chicago talk about my "life force," but at that point, beggars couldn't be choosers. So my attitude was "Reiki away."

This is not a condemnation of Reiki or any other alternative therapy, but in this case it did jack shit. My pain only got worse. Eventually I went into the bathroom and tried to make myself throw up. I couldn't. I just lay on the floor and moaned louder and louder. By four in the morning nothing had changed except the intensity of pain, and we decided it was time to go to the emergency room. I think in the back of both of our minds we still thought it was something small and we'd just be wasting money. But I was in so much pain, I was willing to pay anything to make it stop.

Denise drove and I took my second backseat ride of the night. I don't recall walking into the emergency room or checking in. What I do remember is lying on a gurney or bed and the doctor injecting the painkiller. Ahhhhhhh. It felt so good to have that agony stop. There is definitely something about pain that makes you feel alive. That being said, feeling alive is overrated.

I'm not sure if the talk with the doctor about the pain, location, and intensity came before or after the painkillers, but pretty quickly the doctor said he thought it was my appendix. I still had mine, and the location seemed to point to that. The doctor told me that the plan was to perform an appendectomy. They'd cut me open and take out my appendix, even if once they got in they determined it was healthy. Now that I was high, I was up for anything they wanted to do. Sure, cut away!

Hours later I woke up in a hospital bed with a curtain pulled around me. I heard people on either side of the curtains. As my senses came back, I figured I was in the ER recovery room. I turned to the side and saw Denise. There is something disconcerting about waking up from anesthesia in a strange room. It's different from waking up from a normal sleep. It's unnerving and scary. A warm look from someone you love helps ease that feeling.

Denise smiled. "How do you feel?"

I was still on drugs. "Good. Really good."

Denise held my hand. We stayed like that for a while, then a doctor came in. He introduced himself as Dr. Daniel Marcus and said he had performed the surgery. I asked how it went. He said it was successful in that they removed the appendix, but there were a couple strange things. First, as they had worried, my appendix was completely healthy. Second, while they were inside me, they noticed something strange on my liver. On closer examination, they discovered nine to twelve tumors.

Denise and I were obviously taken aback. She squeezed my hand tighter. "What kind of tumors?" I asked.

"We're not sure yet," Dr. Marcus said. "We'll run some tests. It will take a couple days for the results. There's nothing to worry about yet. For a few days you'll be sore from the surgery but you can go home in a couple hours. I'll call you when the tests come back."

Before he left, I asked the million-dollar question: "If my appendix was fine, where was all the pain coming from? Was it these tumors on my liver?"

Dr. Marcus said, "No, the severe discomfort wouldn't have been coming from there. Truth be told, we don't know what caused the pain. But the good news is that it got you in here and allowed us to discover what was going on with your liver. We'll talk in a couple of days."

If there was a bright side to the surgery, it was that I was pretty doped up over the next few days while we waited for the results. It was really easy to stay positive while intoxicated on painkillers. I was thirty-four. What were the chances the tumors would be anything serious? They had to be low. I was young. I was in good shape. I had never had a serious health problem my entire life. There was no history of cancer in my family that I knew of. Denise echoed my logic. Although she wasn't on drugs, so maybe she was just putting on a brave face to make me feel better. If that was her plan, it worked. The two days of waiting went by pretty quickly.

Denise had taken off the day Dr. Marcus had said he would call. She wanted to be available in case he called us to his office. Dr. Marcus called as he said he would. He was incredibly nice on the phone and said that the results were in but he did not have them. He was referring me to another doctor who specialized in tumors, an oncologist named Orenstein. I knew that was a cancer doctor. Dr. Marcus reassured me that this didn't signify anything about the tests; it was just the best person to analyze the results and tell us what we were dealing with.

I believed him. I had crossed paths with a lot of doctors in my years in the Navy, and few had the sincerity of this guy. I trusted him. If he was telling me there was nothing to worry about yet, I wouldn't. He had made an appointment for me with Dr. Orenstein for the next day. I was still confident everything would be fine.

The only problem was that Denise couldn't take off the next day. There was a big meeting at her job and she had started only three weeks earlier. It wouldn't look good for her to take a third day off so soon. She didn't care. She said her boss would get over it. But I wasn't so sure. The only thing that could make this situation (and this month) worse would be losing another job.

I told Denise not to worry. It was just a meeting with a doctor. He was going to give me some results. I could do that on my own. I was positive it was going to be good news and then it would just be a wasted day for her. I told her to go to work and we'd celebrate the good news when she got home. She agreed on one condition: someone else had to go with me. She didn't want me to go alone. Just in case.

10

Diagnosis Focus

Fine. To make Denise feel better, I'd bring one of my friends. Lee was around and available the next day. He picked me up. The oncologist's office was about ten minutes away from our place, in the Howard Hughes Center. I knew it as an entertainment and retail area. Denise and I went there all the time for dinner or to see a movie. But sure enough, just across the street from all that fun stood a building that housed a bunch of labs and doctors' offices. While I had been having fun, sick people had been going in for health problems. Now it was my turn.

Dr. Orenstein's office was a weird shape. His lobby was like a triangle. I had never been in such a odd-shaped office. I had driven by buildings with strange shapes and edges and wondered how those rooms looked inside, and now I knew: strange. Lee distracted himself with texting and looking something up on his phone. I grabbed a magazine while we waited. Lee muttered something like, "Yeeeah, how you holding up there, Brother?" but he didn't look up from his phone.

Lee has always had a hard time focusing. Gary, Sean, and I teased him a bunch about it. He'd often start conversations and then trail off, or jump back into a conversation that had been over for a few minutes. Lee knew he was easily distracted and was a good sport about the teasing. But I could tell he wasn't really listening for a response to his question, so I didn't give him one.

After about ten minutes, the assistant called my name. Lee and I were ushered through a door and into a waiting room. He said Dr. Orenstein would be right in. I hopped up onto the examination table and started playing with the eye and ear inspectors. Lee just kept texting away.

Dr. Orenstein came in a couple minutes later. I liked him right away. He was a bit older with gray hair, glasses, a white lab coat, and a goofy smile. He looked like Tony Kornheiser from the sports show *Pardon the Interruption*, which is one of my favorite shows and probably why I liked him right away. He introduced himself, and after some small talk, he asked how I had been feeling since the surgery.

"Pretty good, I guess. Still a little sore. Better each day."

"Good. You look good. Healthy."

Then he opened up his folder and started flipping through a bunch of pages. He said these were the lab results for the growths on my liver. I clenched the side of the exam table but tried to remain calm-looking. Lee's head was down into his phone. Dr. Orenstein recited off a bunch of things about the tests and how they were conducted and what we could and couldn't tell from them, but I don't really remember any of that. I just remember at some point he said the words "They are malignant."

I clenched the sides of the table tighter. Had I heard him right? He seemed to fly right by those words. He continued talking, but I had stopped listening. He made eye contact with me and gave me a reassuring look, both sympathetic and friendly. His mouth was still moving and I guess he said some important things, but I was in some spacey, out-of-body place. I felt like I was looking at me looking at him. Lee still fiddled with that stupid phone. How could Lee not even look up when I had just been told I had cancer?

Dr. Orenstein closed the folder. My hearing seemed to return. He said it was too soon to know what all of this means. The one thing he did know was that these types of tumors don't originate in the liver. They were coming from somewhere else in my body.

My first thought was of that old movie where the babysitter is getting threatening crank calls and the police tell her they're coming from inside the house! I imagined my liver answering a phone, "The tumors are coming from inside your body, get out!"

"The first thing we need to do is to run tests to determine where these tumors are coming from," Dr. Orenstein said.

My first appointment was the next day at UCLA.

He then asked if I had any questions. Lee finally looked up. I'm sure I could have thought of some, but I didn't have any right then. Reality was seeping in. If I had one question, it would lead to 400. I felt like I should just go home and think about everything.

Though I had just been told I had cancer, part of me doubted it. The news had been so uneventful. There was no crescendo of music that abruptly ended. No weeping. No hugging. No glasses coming off as the doctor broke the bad news in an uncaring way. Had he really told me the tumors were malignant? He said that word, but maybe it was about what the test couldn't find. It was all so surreal that I felt more in the dark than before I went in.

Lee dropped me off at my place. "Let me know if you need anything at all, Brother."

I needed a friend who paid the hell attention when I was getting an awful diagnosis. Did Lee even know what the doctor had said in there? Couldn't he be focused one damn time?

It was hard to be too mad at Lee, since I was confused about the news myself. But when I relayed the story later to Denise and Gary, they both were shocked about how Lee behaved at the doctor's office. They were so shocked I started resenting him a little bit. As the following months went by, we'd joke about Lee's not paying attention in the office, about what he was looking at on his phone. Once again I was coping about some dark stuff by joking.

"Yeah . . . Hey, excuse me, Doc, have you guys seen this version of Tetris? I got a new high score. . . . Sorry, fellas get back to your diagnosis stuff."

We'd all crack up about it, but it really did bother me deep down inside that he was distracted in those moments. We never joked with Lee about it. He wouldn't have found it funny; rather, he would have thought it cruel. And it was. But laughter helped me deal with the pain of it.

Years later I spoke with Lee about how people ask if I talk about cancer onstage. I told Lee I don't because the minute you tell people you have cancer, they act different. I don't want an audience to pity me or act different; I need to know the laughs are real.

Then Lee said, "Yeah, it's not even the pity. It's just the discomfort of it. People don't know how to react when you hear someone has cancer. I remember when you got your diagnosis; I didn't know what to do. You'd just got the worst news of your life. I couldn't look at you. My best friend has cancer? I wanted to cry. But I wanted to be strong for you. I didn't want to lose it. So I just kept my head down and stared at the blank screen on my phone."

Oooofff. He had been focused the whole time. He was right there with me. Lee hadn't known how to act, just as much as I didn't. I had been so unfair to him and he didn't even know. I felt awful.

That lesson is one I have learned over and over since my diagnosis. I wasn't the only one dealing with cancer. Everyone around me was, too. Denise, my friends, my family. I had the diagnosis, but we were all going through it. Sometimes together. Sometimes individually. Sometimes we dealt with it well. Sometimes not so much.

I considered *that* month one of the worst of my life, but the next month was definitely *the* worst. In addition to having the news soak in, I was busy almost every day getting tests. The doctors were having an extremely hard time finding out where my tumors had originated. I was going to UCLA at least two or three times a week for exams. Denise, Gary, and Lee took turns going with me.

The companionship was great, but I really needed the help, too. Most of the tests involved having to drink some god-awful amount of a gross solution, or having to fast for twenty-four hours. I was woozy and tired. I'm sure I was depressed from the ongoing onslaught of PT scans, CT scans, and blood tests. After not finding anything for three weeks, one test involved sliding a tube with a tiny camera on it down my throat. It was so long it went into my stomach and then into my intestines. I looked like a sword swallower. I had to keep my throat open and was constantly gagging around the tube that kept sliding farther. It went on for almost five minutes. Tears were streaming down my face from the discomfort. I'd say I was crying, but this was something different. Crying involves a sound and breathing. I couldn't do either of those. When it finally was over I felt more exhausted than I have after any workout.

Finally after a month of tests, the source of the cancer was found—the small intestines. It was spreading from there, or metastasizing, to my liver. The next day I was called back to UCLA to meet with a team of doctors to discuss a strategy for dealing with everything happening inside me.

Denise came with me. This meeting was much less personal than the ones I'd had with Dr. Marcus and Dr. Orenstein. We gathered in a big office that looked like a lawyer's conference room with a big desk and nice furniture. Four doctors attended, each had a specialization that related to my diagnosis. One dealt with the liver, one with gastro-intestinal problems, and the other two were general oncologists. They talked as much to each other as they did to us, and sometimes I felt as if they didn't know we were there, even though they were discussing me.

Denise and I were nervous because we would finally learn what we were up against. We knew the tumors on my liver were cancerous, but we didn't know how much danger I was in. Now that they had found the source, Denise and I knew this meeting would tell us how serious my diagnosis was.

One thing was quickly agreed upon by all the doctors: the cancer in my intestines would have to be removed immediately. One doctor said they had already scheduled the surgery for the beginning of the next week. I should probably put that on my calendar.

Then they began discussing the tumors on my liver. This lead to a lot of disagreement. It was strange to listen to very smart people arguing about what to do with my body. At some point the doctors looked at Denise and me and asked what we thought. We looked at each other. I don't think either of us knew what they were talking about. I know I didn't. So I said I didn't really understand what the debate was about.

One of the doctors put it as plainly as he could, which wasn't plain at all. He said I had neuro-endocrine carcinoid tumors on my liver. The debate concerned whether or not to treat my liver during the surgery to remove a foot of my intestines.

"How might you treat it?" Denise asked.

"Chemo and radiation aren't effective on these kinds of tumors. Because of the number of tumors, cutting them off isn't feasible. But we've recently had some success in shrinking tumors using electrolysis," one doctor said.

"Why don't we try that?" Denise asked.

"The procedure is new and not completely proven to be effective to the degree we think is worthwhile," the doctors who didn't agree with this treatment said.

"What is the alternative?" I asked.

The doctors exchanged looks. Finally, one answered, "Just wait."

"For what?" I asked.

"To see if new more proven treatments come up."

"There's no proven treatment now?" I asked.

The doctors again looked at one another. It was like they were wondering who was going to tell us something they hoped we had already figured out. Obviously, Denise and I hadn't.

One of them leaned in and said, "There is no cure or treatment for the type of cancer you have on your liver."

Well, I had been waiting for a big dramatic boom moment, and here it was.

The doctor continued. "That's the bad news. If there's any good news, it's that these tumors are usually very slow growing. The hope is that they grow slow enough to allow us time to discover a treatment or cure."

Denise jumped in. "How slowly do they grow?"

All the doctors shifted in their chairs, indicating there was no easy answer.

"Well, it's hard to tell. We know these tumors are generally slow growing over a period of time. But we are not sure how long they've been there. We don't know their rate of growth right now."

That didn't really tell us anything, but I don't think they knew any more. Denise is a bottom-line person, and she asked what she wanted to know without all the guessing. "How serious is this?"

One said, "The intestinal source is very serious. It must come out right away before things become critical. On the liver side . . . there's no way to tell for sure. We've seen patients your age live ten or fifteen years with these tumors."

Ten or fifteen years? I was thirty-four. They had seen people like me live till they were forty-five or fifty. And they were making that sound like good news? Silence filled the room. While all they'd said was sinking in, another question bubbled within me. Just as it reached my mouth, I looked over at Denise and could see that she had the same follow-up question.

"If ten or fifteen years is the best-case scenario without finding a cure . . . what is the worst-case scenario?"

Again, they all shifted in their seats. Finally, one of them tilted his head and shrugged. "Five years."

Double BOOM. Denise and I were stunned . . . too stunned to even think of any more questions.

The same doctor continued. "We really have no way of knowing. It's impossible to tell how long the tumors have been there already and how quickly they might grow in the future. Not with any certainty."

Denise and I stared at the doctors. Another doctor broke the silence by bringing us back to the question as to whether or not the surgery to remove the section of intestine would involve any liver procedure. Again one of the doctors reiterated that the procedures available weren't proven and we should wait.

The doctor who specialized in liver problems said that the one benefit of attempting some type of experimental procedure, even if it didn't do any good, was that it would then count as a "liver procedure," which would help if I ever wanted to get on the liver donor list. He could add to our team of doctors at the surgery a colleague who had some pull with the liver donor list. The other doctors seemed to agree.

I had no idea that the official liver donor list was so political. So much so that it might pay to have a worthless procedure performed, or a surgeon as a guest at my operation just so his influence was available later. It all sounded crazy. Then again, what didn't sound crazy over this past month?

The doctors suggested we go home and think about it for the night. We could call and give them our decision on the liver procedure in the morning. Denise and I thanked them for their time and headed toward the door. I was in a haze. One of the doctors stopped Denise on the way out and talked with her for a minute or two. I hardly noticed.

Denise caught up to me and we walked to our car in the parking garage without saying a word. We didn't even look at each other. It was a combination of not wanting to make eye contact and being preoccupied with everything running though our minds. The silence followed us into the car. I was driving and pulled out of the garage and drove for a few blocks, still in a daze. We came to a stop sign. Then I slowly turned to look at Denise and we both lost it. I leaned over and started crying on her shoulder, and she did the same on mine. I somehow maneuvered the car to the side of the road and we continued bawling into each other. I was scared and sad. I assume Denise was the same. Neither of us said anything. We just stayed there holding each other as wave after wave of tears flowed out of us. When one of us would die down, the other would take over.

After a half hour or so, we were just resting our heads on each other's wet shoulders and whimpering the way kids do when they cry themselves to sleep. We were exhausted. There was more in both of us but it couldn't come out anymore.

"I love you," Denise whimpered, her head still tucked beneath my shoulder.

"I love you," I answered.

We wiped our faces, pulled back into traffic, and drove home.

11

In Good Hands

My operation was scheduled for a Monday. That same week I was scheduled to perform at one of my home clubs in San Francisco, the Punch Line. I was featuring there by this time, even though I had left as a host. I guess some time away had allowed them to see that I had grown in the craft. A week of comedy at Punch Line started on Tuesday and ran through Saturday. Obviously, having major surgery on Monday would keep me from being there Tuesday. But I needed the money. My medical bills from the tests were already mounting, and the last thing I could afford was to miss a week of work.

I called up the manager-booker, Molly, and told her that I was going in for surgery. I thought I would still be able to make it by Thursday if she could find a local replacement for Tuesday and Wednesday. She totally understood. She only asked that I let her know right away if for some reason I couldn't make it. I told her I needed the money and would be there for sure by Thursday.

Of course I didn't make it. Not even close. I didn't even get released from the hospital until Sunday. It's laughable that I ever thought I would recover quickly enough not only to be out of the hospital by Thursday but also to drive five hours to San Francisco and then do five comedy shows in three nights.

This was major surgery. I assumed it would be like the appendectomy, which had me home twenty-four hours later and up and around within forty-eight. This was a much bigger operation, which removed a foot of my small intestine. The surgeons located the cancer and then gave themselves enough room on each side to make sure they removed it all.

We decided against the experimental liver procedure, which was the center of the big debate the week before. We weighed all the benefits, and although getting onto the liver donor list early was tempting, the risks were too high. After our meeting with the doctors at UCLA, one of them had told Denise a story about a patient with tumors similar to mine. The patient had electrolysis on them, but during the procedure the liver failed. That patient died on the table. The doctor suggested that since my liver was functioning fine at the moment, we not mess with it. Denise's mind was made up the second she heard that story. I agreed. Rather than be aggressive with the liver, we'd just have the source cut out.

Still, I had been cut open and had a section of a major organ removed. It was an incredibly invasive procedure that left me sore and exhausted. My body was so shaken that I couldn't stand for the first four days, and then I had to basically learn to walk again. My legs worked, they were just so weak that they couldn't support me.

It turned out I had only just gotten out of the Intensive Care Unit by Wednesday. While I was there, Denise called Molly to tell her there's no way I could make the gig. In one of my first lucid moments, Denise told me she called and canceled my week. I was furious. In my anger I conveniently passed out for another fourteen hours.

I remember only flashes from that week in the hospital. I can recall having a few visitors in the Intensive Care Unit: Denise, Lee, my friend Sue Nelson, and another comedian Dave Kessler. Once I was moved out of ICU to a regular room, I remember a lot more. Gary, Sean, and, most of all, my mom.

Once the surgery had been scheduled, my mom immediately booked a flight to Los Angeles. All the visitors were a blur except for Denise and my mom. I have very distinct memories of them taking care of me at the hospital. Truthfully, I think the other visitors just made me tired. Of course, I was happy they were there. They cheered me up. But seeing a friend looking down at you, smiling and making jokes, you naturally want to engage them. You want to respond. You want to let them know how much you appreciate their being there. But I was so weak that even after ten minutes of just having someone new in the room, I was ready for a long nap.

At one point, five or six people were in my room. One second I was happy to have them there, and the next I was so drained I needed Denise to ask everyone to leave. It's funny because in normal life, I never want people to leave. I always want people over at our house and love it if they stay into the wee hours of the morning. Denise, on the other hand, has a cut-off where she's had enough fun and wants her house back to herself.

The two people I wanted to stay all the time was my mom and Denise. A couple times I woke up and they were not there because visiting hours were over. It was unnerving. I felt so alone. So sad. The room was cold and quiet. I think Richard Pryor said it best in one of his comedy specials, "The hospital ain't no place to get better."

As much as I loved having my mom and Denise there to take care of me, it was hard on both of them. First, they had to constantly look at their loved one lying in a hospital bed, tubes poking out of several places, and going in and out of consciousness. My mom saw her son in the worst possible condition. Denise saw her boyfriend fighting cancer. It could not have been easy to deal with, let alone to put on a happy face for me.

On top of that, there is always that weird mother-girlfriend dynamic. Mothers feel like they know what's best for their sons because they've raised them. The girlfriend thinks she knows best because she is taking care of the son now. It's like a torch is supposed to be passed, but neither lets go of it.

Mom was uncomfortable about stepping on Denise's toes when it came to taking care of me. She was apprehensive about taking control, and I understand why. Denise is a take-charge person, and she felt like she knew best what I needed. But she was my girlfriend of just eight months, so I'm positive my mom wanted to make sure I was in good hands. I was.

Together, along with the nurses, Denise and my mom helped me get better. They fed me, played games with me, watched TV with me, and just sat on the bed as I went in and out of sleep. They both helped me take my first wobbly steps, to the bathroom I think. Then we slowly ramped up and started taking short walks to the nurses' desk and back. Within a couple days we were doing laps around the recovery ward a couple times a day.

Overall, it was an awful time. The pain. The fatigue. The knowledge that this was all related to an incurable disease that could put me back in the hospital at any time. The realization that I might have only a few years to live. I felt like a cancer patient that week in the hospital. But amidst all the fear, doubt, and uncertainty, I was also given an incredible memory.

One time I woke up and woozily looked around the room. I saw my mom sitting in the chair, reading. My mom loves to read and goes through two or three books a week. It felt good to see her there, but she hadn't yet noticed I was awake. I didn't have the energy to say anything, so I just watched her. It had been a long time since I'd really looked at my mom.

Kids have a picture in their minds of their parents at a certain age and that's the vision that sticks with them. If a police sketch artist told me to describe my mom, I'd probably describe her when she was in her forties. That's how I remember her. She was in her mid-sixties by now and looked great. She has a young face. But it was her eyes that caught my attention. It's strange how the rest of our bodies age, but, for the most part, our eyes stay the same. The skin around them might sag or wrinkle, but the eyes themselves remain unchanged. My mom's eyes were a beautiful blue. I focused on them. I had never noticed how blue they were. When she looked up, she saw me staring at her.

When she realized I was awake, she closed her book and came to my bedside. She asked if I needed anything. I shook my head. She sat down on the side of the bed and grabbed my hand. And she just held it.

I think she knew I was still too out of it to talk. She didn't say a word. We just sat there holding hands. It felt strange and familiar at the same time. I'm sure I hadn't held her hand since I was a little boy. After the age of ten I would have been too embarrassed to be seen holding her hand, and as an adult there was no reason to. If I walked somewhere with her, she'd often take my arm, but never my hand. So her hand felt foreign to me. It wasn't the tight skin of a mother in her thirties that I remembered as a kid. Her hands and mine were much older now. I'm sure mine felt just as peculiar to her; no longer small and smooth like a child's. But hers was as tender and caring as it had been decades earlier. And it was what I needed. It felt good. It felt safe.

12

Reality Sets In

A week after the operation I was back home, recovering in my own bed. Being home helped a lot. My mom stayed in town for a couple days and helped out when Denise was at work. Denise had also asked Lee, Gary, and Sean to check in on me as much as possible. I spent very little time alone, and that was probably good. There was no time to wallow in self-pity and be depressed.

It took me a couple weeks to get my energy and strength back. As my body healed and I stopped taking all the painkillers, my head cleared up, too. Reality slowly seeped in. Medical bills began arriving from the first emergency room visit and surgery, followed quickly by the invoices for the month of tests I went through. The postal service was a daily reminder that I had cancer. If I woke up and got through a couple hours without thinking about it, the mail slot would pop open and a reminder bill would land of the floor of my living room. The dachshunds would bark at the mailman and slide around on the envelopes. Their barking was like a twisted AOL notification. Instead of "ruff-ruff" I heard "You've Got Cancer!"

Eventually, I was completely healthy again. Well, except for the fact that I had tumors growing all over my liver. But if you met me on the street, you'd never know I had cancer. You couldn't see my tumors. You couldn't see the scars on my belly from surgery. I looked like a healthy man in his thirties. But I knew—I knew what was going on inside me. I knew the best- and worst-case scenarios.

The healthier I got, the less I needed to be cared for or checked up on, and the more time I spent alone. The more time I had to not be distracted. The more time I had to think about my diagnosis. My future. Denise's future.

Denise had been amazing from my first pains all the way through the surgery and recovery. We had known each other for only eight months. We were still in that honeymoon phase where everything was perfect when it all hit the fan. A lesser woman would have stepped to the side and let my family handle everything. Denise didn't step aside, she stepped up. She took control, and took care of me like someone who had been with me for a decade. I loved her before the health problems, and that love had grown enormously.

I was lucky to have Denise. If I hadn't been with her, I'm sure I would have ended up back in Chicago living with my mother and having her take care of me. I would have basically been out of comedy.

One night Denise and I lay in our bed and made a list of all the terrible things that had happened in the couple months since we'd moved in together: the cancer diagnosis, the car accident, her old job, Lexie getting sick, and a bunch of other things I am thankful I can't recall now. I do remember the list had about thirty items on it, taking up almost the entire sheet of lined paper. I know that because when I was in grade school and got in trouble, I'd have to write sentences 100 times. And I remember getting about thirty on a page. When Denise and I thought we had put down every last horrible thing, we took the list out to our backyard and burned it.

On top of having deeper feelings for Denise, I started feeling bad for her. Here was this wonderful woman in her mid-thirties. Beautiful. Caring. Ambitious. Strong. Everything going for her. A catch in anyone's book. But now she's attached to some guy who might not be around in five years. The same five years that are pretty important in a woman's life if she is looking to start a family. Can she afford to continue a relationship that might end with her alone in a few short years? Can she start a family with that guy? Does it make any sense, at this early stage, to continue forward with someone with this diagnosis, no matter how she feels about him?

I can tell you, I'm not sure I would have been as strong as Denise. I loved her, and if she had gotten sick I would have taken care of her, but I honestly can't say that I would have stuck around to see how it all played out. What was the point of planning a life with someone who might not be able to share it?

Denise was a better person than I. I'm sure she had thought, "What the hell did I get myself into?" If she did, she never let me know. Of course, this made me love her even more. She amazed me at each step. But all this love and amazement made me feel bad that she was even in this awful position with me. Why should someone as incredible as her be put in this position?

I didn't think it was fair. She shouldn't have to make such a weighty decision of whether to stay with me, not knowing what was going to happen, or leave me while I fought my cancer alone and feel guilty about it. She was in a terrible predicament, and I had put her there. Rather than put her through all this, I decided to make the decision for her. I decided the right thing to do, the fair thing to do, was to tell her I didn't want her as my girlfriend anymore.

13

Message in a Bottle

So I asked her to be my wife.

Come on, I may have been sick, but not sick in the head! That's what I had to have been for thinking—even for one second—of cutting Denise loose. I had cancer, I wasn't crazy. Ultimately, I could not deny what a great woman I had found in Denise. And no matter how unfair I thought her predicament was, I didn't have the right to make a decision for her. I didn't want to let her go. I couldn't. If she decided she wasn't up for sticking around for an uncertain future, I'd understand, but it would be her call. I loved Denise. I needed her. I wanted her to know that, despite whatever she was feeling, I wanted her to stay. For the future. For the five years. For ten years, or twenty, or fifty. Whatever time I had left, I wanted us to be together.

I proposed to Denise at the top of the John Hancock Tower in Chicago. She said yes! Actually, she never did say yes. But I knew she meant yes.

The summer of 2005, six months after my diagnosis, I was working at Zanie's Comedy Club in Old Town Chicago. Zanie's has a great apartment for the comics, just a block from the club and a short walk from Lake Michigan. Comedy Condos usually suck, but this was one of the good ones. Denise was flying in and I was going to take her to all the great places in Chicago. At least this is what Denise thought she was coming to town for.

Earlier in the week I called my old college friend Mary and told her I was going to propose to Denise. She knew all that Denise and I had been through and was excited for the both of us. She asked if Denise had any idea of what I was planning. I told her no, I was pretty sure Denise thought we'd never get married.

Even before my diagnosis, I told Denise that I never wanted to get married again. I might spend my life with one woman, but I didn't see any need to marry her. My cancer had only cemented that belief. Why would I marry someone who would be stuck with all my medical debt? Why not just love and live together?

Denise and I argued a lot about this. She understood, of course. She knew that once she was my wife, she'd be legally tied to all my problems. But she wanted in. Denise complained about not being privy to medical information because she was my girlfriend. She said she needed to be my wife, that there was a big difference. I didn't see it, but she did. If she was sticking by my side and going through all this, the least I could do was make our partnership official. Having a piece of paper making our life together legal meant nothing to me, but it meant a lot to her. Denise meant a lot to me. In the end it was an easy decision.

So Mary asked how I was going to propose to Denise. I was going to do it at the top of the Hancock building. Mary was from Chicago and agreed it was a great idea. Then she wanted to know if I had a ring. I didn't and needed her advice in choosing a ring.

I had no money for a ring. Not a nice one. Not even a not-so-nice one. The medical bills had been piling up over the summer. In less than half a year I was $40,000 in debt. And I had more check-up scans scheduled, which would add more bills. I was barely staying afloat. How could I spend money on jewelry when I still owed doctors who saved my life? I asked Mary if I could just get a cheap, $20 band from a department store near my mom's house. Although Mary offered to lend me the money to get a decent ring, I couldn't do that. I appreciated her generosity, but what I did need from her was her opinion if it would be okay to give Denise a cheap band with a promise to get her the incredible ring she deserved when we could afford it. Mary assured me it would be more than okay.

I had my mom's car for the weekend, so my plan was to pick up Denise from the airport on Saturday morning and head right into the city. We'd drop her bags at the Comedy Condo and then go for lunch. After lunch I'd take her up to the lounge at the top of the Hancock and ask her to marry me. I had it completely mapped out.

Except for the part where I lock the keys in the car the night before.

After my show on Friday night, my childhood friend Aaron, his brothers, and I went out for a beer. I tossed my backpack in the car—I planned on sleeping at my mom's place that night. The ring and a few other things I needed were at my mom's, too. When I threw my bag into the car, I unknowingly dropped my keys in, too. I hit the door lock.

Two hours later I noticed. By then it was after 2:00 AM. Denise was arriving in less than five hours. In that time, I needed to get in the car, drive an hour into the suburbs to pick up the ring, get some rest, and then drive back to O'Hare airport to pick up Denise. Just as I didn't have money for a ring, I didn't have money for a locksmith.

Luckily, Aaron and his brother, Jeremy, had just left. I called them and begged them to come back and pick me up. They also lived in the suburbs. When they came back, I pleaded with Jeremy to drive me to my mom's place to pick up a spare key and then drive me all the way back into the city. Jeremy must have a soft spot for love because he agreed right away.

A little after 5:00 AM, Jeremy dropped me back at my mom's car. Rather than try to squeeze in an hour of sleep, I figured I should just stay up. I grabbed some caffeine and headed for O'Hare. Thankfully, Denise didn't get any sleep on her flight. I was happy to hear that. She seemed suspicious about my joy over her lack of sleep.

"Let's go the condo and take a long nap, then go see the city."

"Why are you so tired?" Denise asked.

"Some friends had come out to the show and we stayed out way too late."

"Why would you do that when you knew I'd be arriving early the next morning and we had planned to spend the day touring the city?"

I was so tired. Lack of sleep had me on edge. It took all my energy not to snap and yell, "Because I was driving all over this damn city trying to find spare keys and a ring so I could ask you to marry me! Are you happy?!"

Instead I just shrugged. "I'm sorry."

If I was gonna get married, I might as well get used to apologizing.

We went back to the condo and slept till about 2:00 PM. I worried about getting over to the Hancock and getting in everything I'd planned to do before my show. Denise would want to eat. She can be very dramatic if she goes too long without eating. If it's lunch and she hasn't eaten, she says she's starving and is going to die if she doesn't get some food. She's not being sarcastic or funny, she really believes it. My show was at 8:00. If we stopped to eat, we might not be able to squeeze in the Hancock trip. Denise isn't the type to grab a quick bite and run. Especially when she's on vacation. She likes to find the right food, then sit down and enjoy it.

Maybe it was payback for the terrible night I had, but when I suggested we just go right to the Hancock and possibly get a snack there before eating, Denise quickly agreed. Things went smooth from there.

The John Hancock Tower is over 100 stories high. It's only a few feet shorter than the tallest building in Chicago, but it has a better view. There is a public viewing floor that you have to pay to get to, but one floor above that is a bar and lounge. If you are going to the bar, you take a different elevator and don't have to pay. That's where we went.

The walls of windows allow a spectacular view of the area. It was a beautiful day, and you could see forever. The city stretched out in three directions, the beach and lake in the other. It's was breathtaking, and Denise loved it. We grabbed a couple of seats by a window. Denise immediately picked up a menu. They didn't offer much, but she found chips and guacamole on there and we ordered some.

I went to the bar and ordered a couple of drinks and the appetizer. Then I leaned in to the bartender and gave him a ten dollar bill and asked him to do me a favor.

"What?" he asked.

I pulled a tiny bottle out of my shorts pocket and handed it him. It was like a clear perfume bottle. I handed it to him. "When you bring our food, please bring this to that young lady."

He smiled and nodded.

Denise and I stared out the window and pointed out all the cool stuff we could see in the city. I was so nervous, knowing what was coming. Of course, Denise had no idea. It was probably good that she was tired and hungry, so that she didn't notice how anxious I was. It seemed like our food was taking forever to arrive. How long does it take to put chips and guacamole in a basket?

Finally, I saw a waiter heading our way. I tried not to smile too big. The waiter put the chips down and then placed the bottle in front of Denise and walked away. Denise picked it up right away. "What's this?"

She thought it was a knick-knack the lounge gave with every order—a cool way to deliver the check or something. The bottle was empty except for a note inside. The note was tied to a string that came out the top under the cap. Attached to the string was a tag that read OPEN ME. When she pulled off the cap, the rolled-up note fell out. She unrolled it. The note said:

Baby,

This is like a message in a bottle.

Because I was lost before I found you.

Now we are here together in one of tallest buildings in the world.

And I don't ever want to lose this feeling.

Say that you'll spend the rest of your life with me and I'll live the rest of mine feeling like I'm always on top of the world . . .

Denise looked up from the note. She had tears in her eyes but still didn't realize I was asking her to marry me. I stood, came over to her, and knelt. I looked up at her and said, "Baby, will you marry me?"

She smiled bigger than I had ever seen. Her eyes welled up even more. She reached down and hugged me. Some people who had noticed what was going on applauded. We exchanged I love yous. When we finally broke our hug, we held hands and just smiled at each other.

"I'm so happy," Denise said.

"Me too."

14

My Next-to-Perfect Wedding Day

Denise and I decided to get married in Las Vegas. We both had been married before and were well beyond organizing a series of events that would only stress us out. Plus, we had no money. That's the real reason. Onstage I tell audiences we got married in Las Vegas because what happens in Vegas stays in Vegas! I'm a single man everywhere else I go. Audiences love that joke. Denise hates it.

Because we were so far in debt with medical bills, we had no money to spend on even the smallest of weddings. The comedy gods lent a hand when I got booked in Vegas for a week of shows. I'd have a free hotel room for an entire week at the Riviera Hotel & Casino. Sin City's known for its quick, easy, and relatively cheap weddings. It seemed like fate. Surprisingly, Denise agreed.

Once Denise was on board, I started imagining a drive-through wedding, or the classic Elvis impersonator minister. I figured if we're doing it in Vegas, let's go all the way. Denise was not on board for that. She ended up organizing the least Vegas-style wedding possible. She found a small very respectable place called The Little Church of the West. It looked like a tiny wooden chapel you'd see in a fairy tale. Nothing flashy about it. It was tastefully decorated with old pews and nice flowers. The people who worked there were "normal" and wore nice suits. It was awful.

No one dressed like Elvis, or the Rat Pack, or Marilyn Monroe. Denise forbid me from dressing like any of them, too. Instead I wore a burgundy blazer Denise bought me for Christmas, a nice shirt, and khakis. Comfy and smart. Denise wore a beautiful gold wedding dress she found on sale. Even our friends dressed respectably. Who were these people?

Since we planned the wedding around the week I was working, setting a date that worked for everyone was impossible. So half of my family couldn't make it. My mom was on a trip to China with a friend, and my sister was living overseas in Japan and couldn't get back. So that left my brother and my dad.

Most of the week, it was great to have my dad in town. He's never a guy to come out and say "Well done" or "I'm proud of you." But he's such a Vegas lover that it was a big deal for him to drive down the Strip and see my name on the Riviera's marquee. I don't know that I could do more in comedy to impress him. On top of that, the Chicago White Sox, the team he had raised me to root for, were in the World Series. We watched a couple of games together and saw them win it all. It was great to have him there.

Until the wedding day.

The one silly thing Denise and I did do for the wedding was write our own vows using only song lyrics from songs we loved. We thought it would be fun for us and those who made the trip out. We even gave the minister a couple of lyrics to get us started. This is how the vows went (I'll let you figure out the songs):

MINISTER

Dearly Beloved, we are gathered here today to get through this thing called life . . .

As with their lives in the past year, Denise and Steve always try to have as much fun as possible. So when they sat down to write their vows they quickly realized that everything they wanted to say to each other had already been written. Not by poets, playwrights, or lovers . . . but by rock stars . . .

STEVE

Denise, before I met you . . . I thought I would be single for the rest of my life; I didn't think I needed a woman. I thought I could live without . . . lovin', touchin', squeezin' . . .

The first time ever I saw your face . . . I felt the earth move under my feet . . . and I realized that you're more than a woman. . . . You're once, twice, three times a lady. . . . You tried to keep your distance, but I knew I've got to get you into my life.

DENISE

Steve, before I met you . . . I thought love was only true in fairy tales, meant for someone else, but not for me. But then I met you and I felt like I've got two tickets to paradise. . . . You're the best listener that I've ever met.

You're my best friend

Best friend with benefits

And now I want to kiss you all over.

STEVE

You did . . . and you shook me all night long.

Friendship, trust honor respect admiration

This whole experience has been such a revelation.

I told my friends, she's my cherry pie . . . my pretty young thing . . . and Denise, you're a hot child in the city . . . that's what I like about you.

DENISE

You are the bearer of unconditional things.

You held your breath and the door for me.

Thanks for your patience. . . . I realize now that I was looking for love in all the wrong places. . . .

Loving you is easy because you are beautiful . . . inside and out. (Whoa, whoa, yeah, yeah.) I love you more than I can say.

STEVE

Baby, I'm amazed at the way you love me all the time. Baby, I'm amazed at the way I need you. And I realized that . . . we are the world. We are the children. We are the ones who make a brighter day so let's start living.

And then I knew I wanna rock with you! And now that you've given yourself to me, God only knows where I'd be without you.

DENISE

We've only just begun and have already traveled a long and winding road.

You think I'd leave your side, baby?

You know me better than that.

Love, love will keep us together.

You're the one that I want.

I am hopelessly devoted to you.

STEVE

You are the woman that I have always dreamed of, I knew it from the start. . . . There's no one like you. . . . I want to stop the world and melt with you.

I just want to be your everything.

MINISTER

I now pronounce you man and wife. . . . You may kiss the bride.

Now it's time for you all to go and do a little dance . . . make a little love . . . get down tonight.

That's how our vows were supposed to go that Saturday morning of our wedding. I don't know if my dad had been inspired by seeing a comedy show, or it was just the six-pack he had gone through already, but he decided to heckle at the wedding. Yes, heckle. That's the best I can describe it. Somewhere in the middle of our vows, he started yelling things out.

Our friends and family were cracking up at the recognition of lyrics as we recited them. But when I said, "I felt the earth move under my feet," my dad yelled something like, "Maybe it was just an earthquake."

The worst thing that can happen is for a heckler to get a laugh. It makes them think people want more. And they oblige. Half of the wedding guests laughed when my dad interjected that. But most of the laughter was out of shock that he did it. Denise and I were facing each other, holding hands. I turned and smiled at my dad, but stared a couple seconds longer to send the message not to do it again. I have a short temper and didn't want to lose it in the middle of our wedding.

We continued on, and I thought he got the point until Denise said, "I want to kiss you all over," and my Dad shouted, "Can we watch?!"

All right, that is about seven kinds of wrong: the occasion, the setting, the relationship between us all, the people in attendance . . . This time it got groans and gasps like a vile joke at a club would. I whipped my head around and was about to lose my temper when I felt Denise's hands squeeze mine tighter. I gave my dad a serious look and said, "We'll handle the comedy up here, thank you."

We returned to our vows, and I did my best to let the boiling inside me simmer down. Thankfully, he didn't jump in again. I'm sure it was because his girlfriend, Barb, had a nail file to his crotch.

After we were pronounced man and wife, we went outside to take pictures with everyone. My dad didn't come by to apologize, and I didn't search him out for a picture. It took a while for that to blow over.

The important thing was that Denise and I were married. All of our guests joined us for lunch and an afternoon party at our suite at the Riv. I had shows that night, but afterward Denise and I stayed the night in a great room at the Bellagio. Her former roommate, Deva, had booked it as a present. Despite a couple of minor speed bumps, it was a great day. I married the woman I loved, shared some time with my closest friends, and did two comedy shows. Pretty close to a perfect day.

15

That First Year

Meeting Denise and then marrying her were highlights of my life. It felt great to have someone so incredible in my corner. But the realities of living with cancer quickly closed in on me. My check-ups were coming back good, but the bills that followed them weren't. Denise and I weren't even close to paying off the first trip to the emergency room.

Every three months I had to visit my oncologist, which included lab work and scans to make sure the tumors on my liver weren't growing too rapidly and that nothing had returned in my intestines. Every doctor's appointment was stressful on Denise and me, both financially and emotionally. We knew they would result in more bills, and feared they'd result in bad news. Luckily, during that first year, all the bad news was financial.

The first year. It hit me. One year had passed. I felt good, but one year had gone by. One year out of the short five I might have left. I had been so busy with all the appointments, the wedding, and trying to book enough comedy gigs to stay afloat, that one year had flown by. I blinked and it was gone. The worst year of my life had also been the quickest.

I guess having your worst year fly by is a good thing. But that year was spent dealing with everything that was happening to me. It was coping with circumstances that had been thrust upon me. I was reacting to life. I felt like I had no control of it. As bad as the year was, I also had some awesome things happen in it. Some incredible memories. I wanted to take control and create many more great memories with whatever time I had left.

Denise and I started to talk a lot about life. About purpose. About dreams. About all the dreams I ever had in my life. All the goals I had thought I had plenty of time to reach. There were so many things I had told myself would happen someday. Now I wasn't sure I was going to be around for someday.

I couldn't sit around and wait for those dreams to come true.

One day while on a drive, Denise said, "I'm confident they are going to find a cure and that you'll die of old age. But if you really had only five years left, what would you want to make sure happened in that five years?"

I knew the answer before she finished the question. I wanted to perform my comedy on the *Late Show with David Letterman*. Denise broke a smile and said she knew that would be my answer. Of course she knew. Even from those early phone calls from road gigs when I first met her, we had told each other about our biggest goals. Hers was to open her own studio and mine was to be on *Letterman*.

It even creeped in when we weren't discussing our goals. One time, a few months into the relationship, Denise wished we could escape away on a trip together. She asked me, "If you could be anywhere, where would it be?"

I'm sure she expected me to describe a deserted sandy beach with beautiful blue water. Instead, I answered, "In New York at the

Ed Sullivan Theater, where I would be performing and killing the audience on the *Late Show*."

Even my romantic fantasies somehow involved David Letterman.

Letterman was one of the biggest reasons I became a comedian. I was twelve years old when his first late-night show premiered, and I was hooked. My parents didn't get his sense of humor, which made me like him more. He was weird, awkward, and dry. Kinda like me! I loved him and the stand-up comics he had on his show. I told myself, *Someday you're going to be one of them.*

But Denise was right. Even if I did beat my diagnosis, I couldn't keep going through life waiting for things to come to me. Forget cancer. I could get hit by a bus long before the five years were up. I wasn't guaranteed any time. I needed to shape the life I had left. I couldn't sit around waiting for someday anymore.

I'd been fortunate to live my life my way: touring the world, working in comedy clubs, and marrying the greatest woman I'd ever met. I was lucky to have more time to chase the things I hadn't accomplished. I renewed my dream to perform on Dave's show. Rather than wait for them to hear about me, I decided to pull out all the stops and do whatever I needed to get on. I was going to make someday happen.

In February of 2006, with my newfound purpose and passion, I gave myself one year to get on Letterman.

The Top 10 Benefits of Catching Cancer

#10 Only seven Tour de Frances away from being just like
       Lance Armstrong

#9 Get deciding vote on which movie or restaurant to go to
      because . . . I have cancer

#8 Can stand as close to the microwave as I want

#7 On the bright side, might be able to finally shed that last
      ten pounds

#6 Can easily top most people's "Awful Day" stories at par-
      ties

#5 Spending the rest of life with just one woman doesn't
      seem so hard anymore

#4 Everyone acts a little nicer to you because they're afraid
      you are gonna die and tell God bad things about them

#3 Blame hair loss on chemotherapy rather than male-pat-
      tern baldness

#2 Two words: Sympathy Sex

And the #1 benefit of catching cancer:

#1 You can convince close friends to work for free

16

With a Little Help from My Friends

The first six years of my comedy career I was confident I'd perform on the *Late Show with David Letterman*. My style of comedy suited the show. I was clean and clever. My comedy was well-written, and didn't rely too much on attitude to sell it. Other comics thought I had jokes good enough to be on the show. I was sure it would happen.

I didn't do much to make it happen except keep trying to get better. Much of the comedy business is just being funny and having people hear about you. That's how I got into most of the clubs, by someone referring me or because a booker had heard I was really funny. So I figured *Letterman* would happen the same way. Eventually I'd get referred to them, or they'd hear about me and want me to audition.

I didn't have time to wait for them to hear about me anymore. Especially, since I had just given myself one year to reach my goal. I needed to make sure they heard about me. I started to brainstorm with Lee and Gary about ways I could make that happen.

The first and most obvious idea was to put up a website where I could share my goal and plan to make it happen within a year.

Even considering this was a big step. Once I put my project on the Internet, I was risking forever being labeled as "that guy who has cancer and is trying to get on *Letterman*." Was I ready for that label? Would it make people feel sorry for me, rather than taking me seriously as a comedian? Did any of that matter if I really believed I was good enough to be on the show? I didn't think so. So I jumped in.

Lee is much more tech savvy than Gary and me, so he started designing a site that described the project. We all agreed that it should have a brief bio of me and an explanation my situation. It should also include a video of my comedy. A sample of me. And pose a question, "Do you think Steve's good enough to be on *Letterman*?" Then it should have a "call to action" where people could help by spreading the word.

This is years before Facebook took off, so we were asking people to tell others by word-of-mouth and e-mailing. We considered starting a petition. We could collect signatures and then send it to the show, demonstrating how many people thought I should be on. Then we realized we should just cut out the middle man. Why not just have a place where visitors could click and it would open an e-mail to the *Letterman* show? We could ask them to send a simple e-mail saying "Book Mazan."

The design of the site came together over a couple weeks. Lee asked if this was just going to be on my personal website, www .stevemazan.com. I thought the project needed its own website. So the new website, and the project, needed a name. I wrote down about a dozen before I came up with Dying to Do Letterman.

It definitely had a ring to it. I thought it was funny. I loved the play on dying. Denise hated it at first because she thought it was wrong to admit I was dying. I told her we were all dying, and this was only saying I really wanted to be on the show. She stared at me like she does when she thinks my point is stupid.

Gary and Lee loved it. Their input and support meant so much early on. I have had a lot of crazy ideas over the years, and they were always supportive. Even if they made fun of me when the ideas failed, they supported them in the beginning. This idea, of starting a campaign to get someone on *Letterman*, was especially crazy. But they helped without batting an eye.

We bought the domain name DyingtodoLetterman.com, and Lee published the site from the office in my backyard. I pulled out my video camera and taped the "going live" ceremony. Our plan was to capture every step of the process and put the videos on the site so people who had helped out could feel like they were taking the ride with us. This was a year or so before YouTube took off, too. Besides the sample of my comedy, I included a video of me explaining the project and giving myself a deadline of getting on the show within a year. The video concluded with me saying, "Let's do it."

Okay, we were live. The project was underway and in cyber-space. I had it linked to my personal website so any of my fans could find it. I also sent out an e-mail to everyone in my address book, announcing the project. It included a link to the site. I didn't mention in the e-mail anything about cancer. I just told people I was giving myself a year to get on the *Late Show*, and if they wanted to help, they should go to the site. They could learn about the diagnosis when they went to the website.

I received an immediate and huge response from my friends, fans, and family. They all wanted to help and offered to spread the word to others. They all sent the show e-mails.

About that same time, I began receiving e-mails from people telling me that what I was doing was inspiring. A lot of them included stories of people they knew who had fought cancer, or were fighting it, with varying degrees of success. Their messages were tender and encouraging. My story and my goal had touched them somehow.

I was humbled. One of my hesitations to starting the project was that it all seemed so selfish. I was asking people to help me reach my dream, but I wasn't giving anything back, except my thanks. Denise would have to make a bunch of sacrifices if I was going to devote all my time to this goal. It was all about me. Yet, somehow people were finding inspiration in my quest. It made me feel better. Up to that point in my life, I don't think I had ever inspired anyone. It felt good. It made me want to get on *Letterman* even more. I felt like I was chasing it for all those people who were inspired, not just me.

Another added bonus was hearing from people I hadn't had much contact with in a while. You know, those friends you talk to every so often, when something big happens, or it's been so long you decide to touch base and catch up? I heard from a lot of those people. Getting cancer is a good way to get people to call you. No one wants to hear you died and say to themselves, "Oops, I owed him a call." Even Joke and Biagio, the couple who had edited my comedy reel, checked in.

Joke wrote me an e-mail saying that she had gone to the website to help out and was shocked to read about the cancer aspect. They were happy to hear I was doing well. It had been a couple of years since I had caught up with Joke and Biagio. They had been busy. Their hard work and talent landed them work on a reality series about Caesars Palace in Vegas called *Caesars 24/7*.

I guess a bunch of people kept leaving the project, and they kept moving up until they were basically running the show. And they were running it well.

It was great to hear about them doing so well. Joke said they had already sent the *Late Show* an e-mail, and wanted to know if there was anything else they could do to help. She and Biagio knew some important people at NBC and could probably help me get on *Leno*. I thanked them but *Letterman* was my dream. I'd hold out.

We were about to hang up when I threw an idea out. "What about helping me make a documentary about my journey to get on the show? I've already been taping some things."

Lee, Gary, and I had thought this might be a logical thing to do with all the videos I was shooting along the way, but I had never considered getting actual documentarians involved. It suddenly seemed obvious. Joke was surprised by the request, but I could tell she was seriously considering it right away. She said that was an interesting idea and needed to talk to Biagio about it. They'd be in touch soon.

The documentary aspect instantly became a no-brainer. If a website was inspiring people, why not have something to show for it all in the end that could continue to inspire? This could be bigger than me. I hoped that Joke and Biagio were interested. I liked them. I knew them. They'd do a great job. But even if they couldn't do it, I wanted to make a documentary about Dying to Do Letterman.

Denise loved the idea of a documentary. She suggested we talk to her boss, too. Denise's boss, Katy, besides owning an acting studio, was also a movie producer. Katy had produced a remake of *Where the Red Fern Grows* with Dave Matthews for Disney. The original was a childhood favorite of mine, and obviously producing for Disney was impressive. Denise would tell her about the project and see what she said.

I was a little worried because when I was going through all the cancer tests and surgery, Katy told Denise not to tell people I had cancer. Katy thought that no one in Hollywood would want to work with me if they knew about my diagnosis. They'd be worried I might get sicker and not be able to work. I'd be a bad investment. It made sense, but it had hurt to hear that. So it seemed a little weird now to pitch a project to her that would be broadcasting my health problems.

Katy thought a documentary was a great idea and was interested in producing it. She had me write down all my ideas for the documentary and come in for a meeting. A week later I was in her office pitching ideas. Obviously a documentary records what really happens, but you still have to have an idea of what you'll be shooting. Would Denise be involved? My friends? My family? If everything happened exactly how I hoped, how would it all unfold?

We talked for an hour or so. Katy could pull some strings and get a camera company to donate some equipment so we could start filming right away. I was excited. It had been only a couple of months and Dying to Do Letterman was taking on a life of its own.

Everything was moving forward. Then Biagio called. He and Joke wanted to meet Denise and me for dinner and talk about the project. We met them at a Mexican restaurant in the valley one night after Denise got off work. I didn't see any conflict of interest at this point. Denise's boss, Katy, was a producer and Joke and Biagio were filmmakers. They could work on this together. That was if Joke and Biagio even wanted to be part of the documentary. They hadn't said so yet.

I'm sure Joke and Biagio wanted to meet Denise and see what kind of condition I was in. Over the chips and salsa, we all caught up on each other's lives. Then we started talking about the documentary. We were still talking about it a half hour after the check came. It was great to see those guys again, and they really clicked with Denise.

They were definitely interested in doing the film. I told them about Denise's boss offering to produce the movie, so they wanted to meet her right away. Since I was meeting Katy the next day, they would come along.

Denise was busy running the acting studio, so it was just me, Joke, Biagio, and Katy discussing the project for almost an hour. It seemed to be going well. At the end of the meeting, Joke, Biagio, and Katy said they needed to talk about some things without me. I understood. I was the subject, not the filmmaker.

That night Biagio called. He and Joke wanted to make this documentary with me, but they didn't think they could do it in conjunction with Katy. They liked her and thought she could do a lot for the documentary. But they were on different pages as far as their approach to making the film. Because they were too far apart, Biagio didn't think it would be best to have them working together on the project. It was a tough decision, but if they were going to make the movie, they needed to make it their way. Biagio said to think about it and let them know.

Wow. I had gone from being ecstatic about how the project was moving to feeling like I was going to vomit because of the choice I had to make. Would I go with my old friends, or would I choose Denise's boss? I couldn't believe I was in this position.

Telling Denise the situation only made it worse. Right away she understood the kind of stress this would cause. She had stuck out her neck for me by even bringing it up to her boss, and now I was considering backing out of working with her. I felt nauseous for a couple days. Probably because I knew the right choice. And Denise wasn't going to like it.

Katy had great ideas and knew a lot of people who could help with the project. But she wouldn't be hands on. She wouldn't have a camera in her hand or be following me around. She'd hire someone to do that whereas Joke and Biagio would do everything: produce, direct, film, and even edit. For a documentary it seemed ideal to have the same people managing all aspects of it. Denise agreed with the reasoning. She felt stressed about the situation, knowing the right decision would be the worst for her relationship with her boss of less than a year. Though an obvious decision, it was not an easy one.

After a few days I called Joke and Biagio with our decision for them to make the film. Biagio asked if we had told Katy yet, which we hadn't. He wanted to meet us for dinner one more time before we told Denise's boss. Oh, no. Were Joke and Biagio backing out now?

I couldn't handle all this stress. Maybe a documentary wasn't a good idea.

When the four of us met at the restaurant, it quickly became evident that Joke and Biagio were still interested in making the movie. Whew. They were happy we chose them but were sorry for having to ask us to make this decision.

Then they got serious. Before we told Katy we wouldn't be using her, they wanted to prepare us for the kind of movie they wanted to make.

"We are your friends. We care about you. But if we are going to shoot this movie, we need to be able to film you even when you don't want us, too. If you're going through something tough, we are going to want to film it. We need it to be real. If you guys are crying, we aren't going to be able to put down the camera and give you a hug like we would as friends," Biagio said.

That they were saying this confirmed to me we had made the right decision.

Joke and Biagio looked at Denise and me with real concern. Biagio finished by saying, "How do you feel about that?"

I grabbed my right side and scrunched my face. "Owwww, you're making my tumors hurt."

They cracked up right away. Denise smacked me on the shoulder, but she was laughing, too. The laughter was just one more indication that they were the right choice. None of us wanted to make a sad sack, sappy movie about cancer. I was a comic. I wanted to face everything with humor. There'd surely be down times, but that's not what we wanted focus on. We wanted to make a movie about dreams.

Right away Joke and Biagio gave me one of two professional cameras they owned. I was to start filming everything, and to do as many diary cams as I could about what I was feeling, planning, and doing. They gave Denise the same assignment. They said they'd be there to film any important news or events, but it would be our responsibility to document all the things they couldn't be there for.

That night I called Katy and explained why I was backing out and going with Joke and Biagio. Thankfully, she understood.

Then I turned on the camera and did my first confessional about the project. We had officially started the documentary.

After a couple of months I stopped receiving e-mails from people saying they had dropped Dave an e-mail. My initial push was coming to an end. I had reached everyone I could through my address book and those peoples' address books. Word had spread, but that spread had stopped.

It made sense. Only so many people were going to stumble onto the site. Honestly, if people were going to do a Google search using "dying" and "Letterman," there was a good chance that something had happened to Dave. In that case, no one would be getting booked.

Getting my project into cyberspace was a great first step. But now I had to go farther. I had to bring it to the real world.

17

Going Public

K enny Kane, who had set me up with Denise, is not your typical stand-up comic. His act is physical and involves dancing, rapping, and usually gyrating on some unsuspecting audience member. He produces a lot of his own shows at the clubs in Southern California. These shows are as skewed as Kenny's comedy. Instead of the typical three-comic show, Kenny includes a musical group, a funny video, sketches, and sometimes even puppets. Just like his own act, Kenny wanted his shows to offer something different.

I had done a bunch of Kenny's shows, mostly as the typical comedian on the roster. Sometimes I'd be part of a sketch, but mostly I did my usual act on his show. But in late 2006, Kenny asked me to be on one of his shows at the Ontario Improv, with the specific purpose of promoting *Dying to Do Letterman*. He wanted to talk to the audience about the project, show the videos from my website explaining the campaign, and then have me perform. Kenny then would ask the crowd to go home and e-mail David Letterman. I thought it was a great opportunity to bring it off the Internet and directly to people. Kenny had great fans and good-sized crowds. It would be the perfect place to take the next step.

There was only one problem. I didn't want to go onstage and perform after people found out I had cancer. If the crowd knew my diagnosis, they would respond differently. I couldn't trust their laughter once they knew. They might just be laughing to make me feel good. Because they felt sorry for me. Pity's the last thing I wanted. So I told Kenny I'd do the show if I could come out and perform first as Steve Mazan, comedian. Then after they had given me an honest response, we could introduce the project and show the videos.

I was nervous that night. There was a really big crowd. It was one thing to put up a website, share my story, and ask for people's help from across impersonal cyberspace. It was completely another to ask people face-to-face. What if I had an off set? Could I give Kenny a quick sign to scrap the whole thing? I couldn't have a crappy set and then ask people if they'd help me get on *Letterman*. I'd already know the answer. There was a lot of pressure

The show started out great. Kenny was hosting the whole night. He ran all over the stage and was doing hip-hop moves for some guy in the front row. People roared with laughter. I was happy the audience was ready to laugh, but Kenny's humor was so different from mine. I wasn't going to dance. I was going to stand still and tell some subtle jokes. I was worried.

Another friend of mine, Eric Toms, was on the show, too. He went onstage in a Superman costume. I don't remember what he did, but it was ridiculous and the audience loved it. The better he did, the more I worried. Eric's set segued into a funny video about a goldfish that ran away. When the video was done, Kenny and Eric went onstage with the goldfish at the end of a fishing pole.

They sang a song with the fish and then Eric left the stage to a lot of applause. I was next.

Kenny introduced me. Immediately his tone and that of the show shifted. Kenny wasn't running around and doing goofy voices anymore; he was being serious. I stood at the back of the room dreading going on. As Kenny wrapped up my introduction I began walking toward the stage. "... please welcome Steve Mazan."

I shook Kenny's hand and grabbed the mic. And I killed. I had a fantastic set. Every joke hit. Hard. The audience was with me right from the beginning and stayed through the end. It felt great. When I was done, Kenny joined me onstage. He took the mic and said, "What did you think of that?"

The crowd gave me another big ovation. Kenny said, "Steve's dream is to be on David Letterman's show. Do you think he's good enough?"

This was followed by another big round of applause. I felt as good as I could about pitching the project to these people. I left the stage as Kenny told the audience he wanted to show them something. A screen dropped down and we showed the videos from the Dying to Do Letterman website.

When the videos were done, Kenny called me back up. The crowd clapped even more. Then he told the audience that we needed their help. "Go to dyingtodoletterman.com and click the 'e-mail Dave' button. How many of you are going to go home tonight and do that?"

Everyone in The Improv applauded, but Kenny and I acted like we were counting individual clappers and pretended like we only got to seven. The crowd laughed, and then I took the mic and thanked them.

As the audience left the showroom, I handed them a little flyer with the web address on it. Some people had to wait in line to get a flyer because people stopped to thank me and give me words of encouragement. I remembered a great joke from one of my favorite comics, Mitch Hedberg. He said that when someone hands you a flyer, he is basically saying, "Here you, throw this away." It is true. Most people hate flyers. But here people waited in line for them. Not for a coupon or to get something for free, but so they could go home and do some work on my behalf. It was unbelievable.

The night couldn't have gone any better. My first attempt at sharing the project live in a comedy club had been a big success. Strangers promised to help me out. I thanked Kenny for all his help and friendship. We were so excited about the response. Still, I tried not to get too happy about the night. I mean, everyone was so supportive and great, but who knew if people were really going to e-mail Dave? And even if they did follow through, who knew if anyone at the show would take notice?

I had an answer to that question pretty quickly.

18

One Step Forward, Two Steps Back

There's nothing worse than checking your e-mail and the only person who sent you a message is some African prince whose family has been overthrown and needs money. It's much better to have a mailbox full of messages from friends and business contacts. The only thing better than that is getting one e-mail you have really been waiting for. Or think you've been waiting for.

A week or so after the show I did with Kenny, I came home late from another gig and opened my computer. When my e-mail updated I saw "The Late Show" in the subject column of my mailbox. I did a double take out of a Laurel and Hardy movie, and reread the entire line:

FROM: Jill Goodwin.
SUBJECT: The Late Show.

I didn't know anyone named Jill Goodwin. The subject line of "The Late Show" was weird, too. Fans or friends had written me about the show, but they always called the show *Letterman* or the *David Letterman Show*. I had a strong feeling that the only person who would call it by its correct name, the *Late Show*, would be someone involved with the show.

I sat on the couch, exhaled, and opened the e-mail. It read:

Hi Steve,

I work at the *Late Show with David Letterman*. If it's ok, one of our Executive Producers would like your mailing address to send you a letter.

Thanks so much,

Jill Goodwin

Jill Goodwin
Assistant to the Executive Producers
Late Show with David Letterman
1697 Broadway
New York, NY 10019

All right. Well. Hmmmmm? Okay. I didn't know what to think. It was definitely from the show. One of the executive producers was asking for something from me. It didn't get much bigger than that. Just Dave himself really. So they knew about me. That was great. My campaign was working. I was excited about that. But not about the rest.

I wanted to wake up Denise. But she was working twelve-hour days with an hour commute on both ends. She was beat. She would be worthless in deciphering the e-mail—if she let me live after waking her up.

I decided to call #2. Gary. He was always up late. I called him and was as cryptic on the phone with him as the e-mail was. "Just come over right away. I need your advice and to film something."

This was a big deal. My first contact with the show. We needed to get it on video. Gary arrived in about fifteen minutes, a speed record for L.A. I opened the door and handed him the camera. I wanted to capture me showing him the e-mail and reading it to him. I think he knew something good must have happened. Although I wasn't sure how good it was.

Gary shot me opening my computer and pointing out that I had an e-mail from a Jill Goodwin at the *Late Show*. I love Gary because he is playful. Sometimes I hate Gary because he is playful. Instead of reacting to the show's contacting me, he said, "I think I once had sex with someone named Jill Goodwin."

"If that is true, I probably won't be getting on the show."

We read the e-mail together, and I could tell that Gary was excited. But just as my excitement waned, so did Gary's. I knew he thought what I was thinking. We agreed that although it was incredible that the show had heard about me, their request for my mailing address probably meant I was going to get a cease and desist letter. Why else would they want my mailing address? To send me a T-shirt?

Gary and I had the same opinion. It was probably for their legal department. If I sent them my address, I'd probably receive something in a few days telling me to stop this whole Dying to Do Letterman project, and citing all the copyright infringement laws I had broken. Still, I had to send them my address. What else could I do? Finally hear from the office of one of the executive producers and then ignore them? Nope. I had no choice. I replied to Jill with my address. I hit SEND and Gary went home.

As sure as I was about the reason for the *Late Show* wanting my address, I still daydreamed it was for something else. Hope springs eternal. As the week passed, I fantasized that an envelope would arrive one day through the mail slot, and the dogs would go nuts barking at it. The show's logo would be on the oversized letter. I'd snatch it away from the dogs, open it, and pull out plane tickets for me and Denise to New York City. There'd be a note telling me what day and time to be there. I knew TV shows didn't handle bookings by snail mail, but I thought this might be a special circumstance. Maybe they'd handle my appearance differently.

I wasn't home the day the letter came in the mail. I opened our front door, pushing a pile of bills across the floor. At the bottom of the pile was the envelope from the show. I saw it right away. It was white, just like the rest. But I was used to seeing the UCLA insignia, or the name of some lab or hospital in the upper left corner. I wasn't used to seeing the *Late Show* emblem, so it struck me right away.

I wanted to rip it open and see what it said. But I had promised Joke and Biagio that I would call them as soon as anything came in the mail. They knew this would be something important, good or bad.

It took our cameraman, Adam, an hour to drop what he was doing and come to my place. That's extremely fast, but it felt forever on my end. Why had I come up with this stupid documentary idea? Adam pulled out his camera. "Let's do it."

I sat on the same couch where I had read the e-mail. I opened up the envelope. No plane tickets spilled out. No schedule was included. There was just a letter on *Late Show with David Letterman* stationary from Barbara Gaines, the Executive Producer of the show. They have several EPs, but she is probably the most well-known. I knew the name right away. At some level it was pretty cool to be getting a personal letter from someone so important. But the cool factor ended there.

Barbara's letter was nice and compassionate. She started by

saying that they had heard about my campaign. (Pause to pat myself and my fans on the back.) Barbara then said she deeply regretted hearing that I was diagnosed with cancer and that she hoped I got better. That lead to her saying she also regretted to inform me that it would be impossible to put me on the show. There was more, but I stopped to reread the word *impossible*. I took it in for a second before continuing.

The letter went on to say that the show received similar requests from people who were sick all the time, and unfortunately they just couldn't honor all those requests. And honoring mine or anyone else's wouldn't be fair to those who didn't get on. Again she apologized but hoped I'd understand.

I understood. I understood completely. They were looking at me as a sick person with a dying wish. A grown-up Make-a-Wish patient. What they saw in my campaign was a person who wanted to be on the show because he had cancer. I didn't. Getting on for that reason would mean nothing to me. I take pride in being honest with myself, and I know when I've received things because I deserved them, and when I haven't. I know how I feel when something isn't deserved. It sticks with me. This dream was too big and meant too much to be reached without being worthy of it. My project was to make some noise and make sure they heard about me. The only reason to consider my diagnosis would be the time frame required for them to look at me. I needed a consideration quicker than usual, because I might have less time. But I did not want to be on the show out of pity.

I understood their stance. If they believed that was what I was asking for, then they should have said no. I wouldn't want to be on any show that said yes for that reason. It wouldn't mean the same. But I also understood, before I even finished the letter, that

I was going to prove them wrong. I was going to show them that I was a talented comic who was qualified to be on the show. Sick or not, I was good enough. I was going to show them that it was *possible*. And when I did get on, it wasn't going to be just for me; it was going to be for all those other people who were told it was impossible.

READER/CUSTOMER CARE SURVEY

HEFG

We care about your opinions! Please take a moment to fill out our online Reader Survey at **http://survey.hcibooks.com.**
As a **"THANK YOU"** you will receive a **VALUABLE INSTANT COUPON** towards future book purchases
as well as a **SPECIAL GIFT** available only online! Or, you may mail this card back to us.

(PLEASE PRINT IN ALL CAPS)

First Name _____ MI. _____ Last Name _____

Address _____ City _____

State _____ Zip _____ Email _____

1. Gender
- ☐ Female
- ☐ Male

2. Age
- ☐ 8 or younger
- ☐ 9-12
- ☐ 13-16
- ☐ 17-20
- ☐ 21-30
- ☐ 31+

3. Did you receive this book as a gift?
- ☐ Yes
- ☐ No

4. Annual Household Income
- ☐ under $25,000
- ☐ $25,000 - $34,999
- ☐ $35,000 - $49,999
- ☐ $50,000 - $74,999
- ☐ over $75,000

5. What are the ages of the children living in your house?
- ☐ 0 - 14
- ☐ 15+

6. Marital Status
- ☐ Single
- ☐ Married
- ☐ Divorced
- ☐ Widowed

7. How did you find out about the book?
(please choose one)
- ☐ Recommendation
- ☐ Store Display
- ☐ Online
- ☐ Catalog/Mailing
- ☐ Interview/Review

8. Where do you usually buy books?
(please choose one)
- ☐ Bookstore
- ☐ Online
- ☐ Book Club/Mail Order
- ☐ Price Club (Sam's Club, Costco's, etc.)
- ☐ Retail Store (Target, Wal-Mart, etc.)

9. What subject do you enjoy reading about the most?
(please choose one)
- ☐ Parenting/Family
- ☐ Relationships
- ☐ Recovery/Addictions
- ☐ Health/Nutrition
- ☐ Christianity
- ☐ Spirituality/Inspiration
- ☐ Business Self-help
- ☐ Women's Issues
- ☐ Sports

10. What attracts you most to a book?
(please choose one)
- ☐ Title
- ☐ Cover Design
- ☐ Author
- ☐ Content

TAPE IN MIDDLE; DO NOT STAPLE

BUSINESS REPLY MAIL
FIRST-CLASS MAIL PERMIT NO 45 DEERFIELD BEACH, FL

POSTAGE WILL BE PAID BY ADDRESSEE

Health Communications, Inc.
3201 SW 15th Street
Deerfield Beach FL 33442-9875

FOLD HERE

Comments

19

Back to Basics

Okay, my campaign had worked. The *Late Show* heard about me. Their response might not have been what I hoped for, but they knew me. Now I had to go back and concentrate on just being funny. I didn't need to spend any more time in organizing stunts to get their attention.

All of my efforts could go into honing my craft. The way to do that was to get back out on the road. In the comedy clubs. Perform night after night to perfect the best set I could, and then somehow get it in front of them. I was excited about the work. The only problem was that this could take a while.

I needed to be as healthy as possible for as long as possible if I was going to change the *Late Show's* producers' minds. Denise had a lot to say on this subject. From the minute I got the cancer diagnosis, she began telling me about alternative treatments she had discovered. I had done my best to ignore her, but I was starting to think that maybe I should listen.

Being sick, and being told I was sick even when I felt fine, was (and is) extra weird for me because I hate all treatments. Even the mainstream ones. I'm sure you're thinking, "Everyone hates scans and surgeries and blood tests." Of course they do. But I even hate taking aspirin when I have a headache. I hate taking any medicine for a cold or fever. I'm very cynical about medication. I figure most problems are solved by resting, eating, drinking fluids, and letting your body do the work to make things better.

Obviously if I broke my neck, I'd let a doctor fix it. I wouldn't walk around with my head on my shoulder waiting for it to get better. And when a treatment or cure is found for my cancer, I'll be there bright and early. I'm just saying I'm hesitant about most medicine. I know everything has an effect—and a side effect. So I'm often suspicious about any treatment.

Denise, on the other hand, is into wacky alternative treatments. You see, she's a California girl at heart. Yoga is probably the most normal thing she's into. She will try everything she reads about, no matter where she reads it. If it's worked for someone, Denise will try it.

At this point I figured I'd try some of Denise's ideas. The first thing she had me do was cleanses. The first one was called "The Master Cleanse." This was a crazy concoction I had to drink for at least ten days. No food, just the crazy concoction. And no other drinks, except water. The "juice" consisted of water, pure lemon juice, maple syrup, sea salt, and cayenne pepper. Sounds yummy, right?

If you were on a cooking reality show and suggested these ingredients, you'd be voted off. Even if you said you were going to combine just two of these ingredients, they'd think you were crazy. "Well, Chef, I've decided to complement the sweetness of the maple syrup with dashes of cayenne pepper. Oh, and to wash it all down, may I suggest this salty lemonade?"

This drink was terrible. However bad you are imagining it . . . it's worse. When I was fifteen, the height of my gross teenage-boy syndrome, I wouldn't have taken a sip of this crap on a dare. Or for twenty bucks. Now Denise had me drinking a gallon and a half of this stuff a day. And nothing else.

The idea is that the cleanse detoxifies your body. The "juice" provides all the basic nutrition you need and allows your digestive system to take a break and purify itself. Among the organs most benefitted are the kidneys and the liver. As a person with problems in my liver, this seemed like a worthwhile attempt.

The first couple days were awful. It's so hard to get used to not having solid food. It's easy to be cranky. The loss of caffeine for me was the worst part. The fourth day is terrible because you really start craving something other than spicy lemons. But after that hump, it gets pretty routine. Your body really does adjust to not eating since it's getting the nutrition it needs.

For me, the hardest part of the cleanse was . . . Denise. To convince me to try it, she volunteered to do it with me. I should have told her I'd do it alone, but I thought it would help to have her taking the ride with me—someone to commiserate with. That was a bad idea. She out-commiserated me by a mile. My crankiness and headaches from the caffeine withdrawal were enhanced by Denise's constant moaning about how hungry she was. If my head was a bell, she would be the mallet.

Denise's favorite activity during the cleanse was to turn on The Food Network and look at all the things we couldn't eat. It was like porn to her—if porn made people angry. I begged her to watch other things, but she'd change the channel back every time I left the room. I don't think I was a good *cleanser*, but I do know that she was a bad one.

Truthfully, I don't know how much purer my organs got as the days passed. But I did feel more energetic. My skin was as clear as it had been in a while. And obviously you lose weight. But that weight comes back pretty quickly once you stop.

That's an important step of the cleanse—stopping. You can't just return to eating normal food. After the ten days, you are to take three or four days to ease back into a healthy diet. I didn't do that the first time. As good as I felt after the ten days, I was ready for some real food on day eleven. I decided to join Lee and Gary at a Denny's after a show they had done. My bad.

I knew not to go too crazy with anything greasy and to watch my portion size. So I ordered orange juice and scrambled eggs with cheese. Well, the eggs weren't the only thing scrambled. My stomach went nuts. No sooner had I taken the last bite of eggs and washed it down when I realized I had better find the quickest route to the men's room. I barely made it. There was no pausing to lock the door or put one of those sanitary toilet seat sheets down. My stomach was evicting everyone, whether they had a place to go or not. There was no sympathy. I suffered for my poor judgment. To be fair, I've heard of others experiencing this at Denny's without going through a cleanse. But I'm positive this one was my fault.

Cleansing was just the tip of Denise's homeopathic iceberg. She also had me visit a variety of experts: an acupuncturist, a masseuse who dealt specifically with cancer patients, a nutritionist who dispensed a selection of vitamins based on how hard my one arm resisted his pressure while I held different elements in my opposite hand, and of course, I participated in yoga and meditation.

I already enjoyed yoga and meditation. I did a lot of yoga in the first few months I dated Denise. To impress her. To court her. I told her I loved it. And I did. But I had the discipline to take class only two to three times a week because I was hot for the instructor. Soon I got to see the instructor every day at my apartment. So I stopped attending classes. Now Denise was pushing me to go at least once a week. I had been doing meditation for years, ever since I lived in San Francisco. Now Denise nudged me to do more.

I tried several alternative treatments, especially in those first couple of years after receiving the diagnosis. But one sticks in my mind more than any other. It was easily the craziest thing I've ever done. It made the cleanse look as normal as drinking milk. It was called Maori Healing.

The Maori (pronounced mow-ree) are an indigenous tribe of New Zealand. They're basically Polynesian. The Maori, I was told, are renowned for their healing practices. Their procedures have been passed down for thousands of years from generation to generation, using an oral tradition. Red Flag #1.

Okay, these traditions have been passed down orally? Meaning the adults told their kids and so on. Have you ever played that telephone gossip game in school? The one where the teacher whispers a phrase in your ear, like "Everyone loves the Easter bunny," and then you have to whisper it to the next person. And that one whispers it to the next. And so on. And then the final person in the line has to say what they heard. By the time it reaches the last player, the message is screwed up. So the last kid says, "Any bum rubs their keister funny."

It's fun. And cute. Cute because it's a silly phrase. It wouldn't be cute if you were passing on important medical information this way. It would be ridiculous.

The Maori have special tribesman who are designated healers. They heal by finding blockages of energy. Blockages of energy apparently cause all disease, complaints, and pain. They believe this happens when the body is not in equilibrium with our feelings. Okay, a little spacey for my tastes, but I'll let it fly.

The healer works on your energy blocks by discovering them through intuition and clairvoyant glances. Let me repeat that. They find the problem through intuition and clairvoyant glances. I'm going to give intuition a free pass and focus just on the "clairvoyant glances." These people are basically psychic. Red Flag #2.

I'm convinced that the only thing these people could tell me about me, just by glancing at me, is that I'm a sucker. But I love my wife; she begged me just to give it a try. This felt alternative to alternative. Denise had heard of people having their cancers cured by seeing a Maori healer, and her best friend had gone to one for help in getting pregnant. The Mother of all Red Flags.

I didn't want to know how he was going to help her get pregnant. But I wanted to know, ya know? I found it silly that the same guy who could help with fertility issues also treated cancer. These guys didn't really specialize. They combined oncology and obstetrics in the Maori tradition, I guess. I just hoped I didn't have to put my legs in stirrups.

There was no need to worry about that. The Maori healer treats you only by waving his hands over your body to give it energy, or by applying pressure with his hands, arms, and forearms. My arms are too tired to wave any more flags. Apparently, the Maori sometimes use a small stone called a *pounamu* to apply pressure as well, because this is what they did to me.

Denise convinced me to go visit these Maori healers when they made a visit to Malibu. I guess they constantly tour the world, and you have to be lucky enough to catch them when they come near you. Like the Harlem Globetrotters.

So Denise and I drove the half hour to some ranch in Malibu where the Maori were seeing people. They had a tent set up that housed two rows of about six tables each. One of the assistants directed me to lie on the table and said the healer would be there momentarily. I lay down and Denise smiled and held my hand. I'm a cynic. But I'm also a romantic. I wasn't doing this for my tumors; I was doing it for Denise.

Most of the other tables were empty. But two of them had patients on them with healers hovering around them, placing their hands a few inches above the patient's limbs, or placing their hands right on them. One of the patients was crying. This surprisingly wasn't a red flag. Denise had told me that the unblocking of the energy sometimes causes people to cry, laugh, or scream. And the crying wasn't out of pain. It was a cry of sadness. I thought it was sad to lose a couple hundred bucks, and I might be crying soon, too.

I didn't share that thought with Denise. I agreed to come, so I should shut up at least while I was here. Plus, my own special healer arrived. He was a big guy. Large and round like an NFL lineman five years out of the league. He had tattoos all over him, even on his face.

Still, he seemed friendly. I liked him. At first. He told me to relax and close my eyes. Denise told me later he just held his hands over several parts of my body. I didn't feel anything until he got to my feet. When he got down there he let out a big sigh. Then he told me to open my eyes.

I looked down and saw him at the foot of the table. He said I was going to feel some pressure. He showed me a small thin stone that was about the length of a toothpick, but twice its thickness. I guess this was the *pounamu*. He then directed me to close my eyes and take a deep breath.

The next thing I know I was screaming at the top of my lungs. Surely my scream sent birds flying from trees miles away. It was excruciating. It was even worse than the pain that had sent me to the ER. It was sharper and more immediate. It was harder. It felt like someone had taken a long carving knife and jammed it into my heel. Jammed it in and kept pushing it in until it was all the way to the hilt.

And then started twisting it.

The healer said calmly above my shrieking, "Let it out."

"Fuuuuuuuuuuuuuckkkkkkkkkkkkk!!!!!!!" I shouted. I wanted to put a "you" on it, but I didn't really have any control.

The F-word trailed into a long, continuous, moaning howl that left my throat raw. It felt like it went on for ten minutes. Afterward, Denise said it lasted only thirty seconds. She also said all the healer did was lightly press on the heel of my foot with the edge of the rock. She swore he put no pressure whatsoever on it, he just touched it to my skin with the same pressure you check someone's pulse.

When he stopped, I rolled to my side and felt exhausted. He told me to rest and that when I felt up to walking, I could get up and come see him at the desk on the other side of the tent. I lay there and stared at the two other patients. They looked at me like, "Check out that pussy."

I thought maybe the healer knew I wasn't taking this seriously and purposely hurt me. Maybe he knew all the smart-ass things I was thinking and made me pay for it. Maybe he was clairvoyant after all.

After five minutes, Denise helped me up. Surprisingly, it didn't hurt at all to put my heel down. I felt pretty good—almost high from the exhilaration of the pain and its alleviation. We met our guy at the desk, and Denise gave him a check. I don't know how much it was for—and didn't want to know. I had been hurt enough. Before we left, the healer gave me a sheet of paper where he had handwritten his diagnosis. I don't know it all by heart, but at one part it said I had a "disease." And then he broke that word in two. Into "dis" and "ease." He wrote that I needed to get back to "ease." To let go of the "dis-ease." I still don't know what I think of that whole day, because it was all so nuts. But I did like that prescription he wrote me. Even if I didn't completely understand it.

Did any of this alternative medicine work? I don't know. I'm still here. Maybe I'd still be here without all of that stuff. But maybe not. The problem with trying multiple alternative treatments is that if you stay stable and healthy, it's hard to figure out which one is working. So you end up just continuing every one of them.

I'll try anything, now. The best that could happen is that I get cured. The worst is that I look like an idiot.

But that's nothing new.

20

Maybe Baby

Kids.

I shudder just typing the word. Don't get me wrong, I love kids. I want kids. I have for a while. But timing has always been a problem. When Denise and I first got together, we were in our mid-thirties and wanted to have a couple of years to do things together before having kids. From our friends and siblings who have children, we knew how much time kids take up. We wanted to make sure we first did everything we couldn't do with kids.

Then I got sick. That changed everything. Being tens of thousands of dollars in debt from medical bills was just one reason trying to have kids seemed like a bad idea. I also had to consider the chance that I wouldn't be around to see them grow up. Even with the best-case scenario the doctors gave me, I wouldn't be around to see my children become teenagers. That made it very hard for me to take that first step. Seeing my child's face would give me incredible joy, but it would also be a constant reminder that I'd never see that face mature. It broke my heart just thinking about it.

Denise had a completely different outlook. First, she thought that having some time with your kids was better than none. Yes, it would be difficult to think about not seeing them become grown-ups, but that wasn't a reason to deprive both of us of the experience of having a baby together. This point was obvious to me.

Denise's next point is one I hadn't thought about, and it went much deeper. If I did die in the next five to fifteen years, I would be leaving Denise alone. She would be left somewhere in her forties, deciding what was next in life. The forties obviously are not the ideal time for a woman to start a new life and just start to consider having babies. It seldom worked that way.

Having kids with Denise would leave her a family. Our family. I may or may not be part of it, depending on what happened over the next few years, but she wouldn't be alone. It was hard to ignore that.

Still, I was less than a year and a half from my diagnosis. There were months we borrowed money from friends and family to keep up with the bills. It didn't feel right to jump into trying to have a baby right then.

At one point I got a call from a bill collector. I told him I was sending everything I could. He asked if I had eaten at a restaurant in the past month. I didn't see where he was going with this.

"I'm on the road a lot for my business and if you consider fast-food places restaurants, then, yes, I have been to a restaurant."

He chuckled, though he obviously was not amused. "Do you think it is fair to be going out to eat when you owe so much money to so many people?"

"I do need to eat."

Silence.

"If I don't eat, I'll probably be dead soon and you'll get nothing."

His only response was a chuckle.

I hung up.

That guy was a douchebag. I'd rather be dead than pay off that guy before anyone else. Denise and I weren't living in the lap of luxury. We were squeaking by and stressing about it. We were cutting corners where we had already cut them. I started helping Gary with a comedy class when I was in town, and even taught Comedy Traffic School. Whatever the opposite of pampering ourselves was, we were doing it.

Still, having a baby did feel like a luxury to me. It was going to be a big expense on top of a bunch of things we already weren't keeping up. It wasn't rent or food. It wasn't something we needed. It was something we wanted. I told Denise we should wait till the following year to start trying to have a baby.

Denise wasn't happy about it. She had a lot of arguments about why we should start as soon as possible. They were good arguments. But I convinced her to wait.

I wasn't scared to have kids. I was scared to have kids right *now*. I already had one big dream underway, and as selfish as it might sound, I felt like our dream to start a family would have to wait just a little longer.

Right now it was time for me to get back to work—to comedy. I hit the road hard, dusting off old bits that I thought might work for Dave's show and writing new ones.

21

Tom Sawyer

I love doing comedy on the road. I've met a lot of comedians who don't like it, which never makes much sense to me. Doing stand-up is basically traveling to different places and telling your jokes; if you don't enjoy that, maybe you don't really want to be a comedian.

One of my friends from San Francisco, a great comic named Dan Gabriel, describes comedians as truck drivers who deliver jokes to cities across the country. That sounds like a great description to me. So if you are going to do stand-up, you'd better like telling jokes *and* traveling. If not, you're like a therapist who enjoys giving advice but not listening to problems.

I knew some great comics in San Francisco who hated going on the road but claimed they loved comedy. I don't think they really did. I think they enjoyed jokes. They enjoyed making people laugh. But stand-up is more than that. It's like music. You can play music in your room, but to become a rock star, you have to go through all the crappy gigs. And even when you get beyond the crappy gigs, you should still like performing. A rock star who doesn't like traveling is a recording artist.

I don't know what a person who can write and tell jokes but doesn't travel is called, but I don't think it's a stand-up comic. I think travel is a necessary element of the job. This isn't to say I don't understand the hatred for bad shows or terrible one-nighters in bars. But I think real lovers of comedy would jump at the chance to perform at a comedy club every week of the year. If not, they thought they liked comedy and learned they didn't.

I love comedy. Like pizza, it's good even when it's bad. I enjoy driving or flying to places I've never been and performing for people I've never met. I like proving to myself that I can make people anywhere laugh. Truthfully, if everyone loves your comedy, your humor is probably a little too generic. But great comics have the talent to win over people who probably wouldn't normally like their sense of humor. The longer I do comedy and the better I get at it, the more people I can entertain. It's bringing the audience with you rather than pandering to it. Traveling the country has given me the skill to do this.

Going on the road was especially nice in those couple years after being told I had cancer. It was what I did before all the doctors' visits, so it made me feel normal. On the road I could leave behind the stress of bills, thoughts about health, and talk about babies.

Best of all, I could focus on what jokes were going to get me on *Letterman*. I could go through my old notebooks and figure out which bits I thought were worthy enough to be on Dave's show. Then I could go onstage and run them, test them, and tighten them. It was fun. I didn't feel sick at all.

In the middle of one of these road trips, I got a voicemail from a number I didn't recognize. I didn't even recognize the area code. I hit PLAY on my phone and couldn't believe who it was and what he was saying. The message was from Eddie Brill, the stand-up comedy booker for the *Late Show with David Letterman.*

I knew Eddie's name. Any comic who wants to be on late night television knows his name. Eddie Brill is a comedian himself and warms up the crowd at the Ed Sullivan Theater before Dave does the show. And on top of that, he keeps his eye on the comedy scene for comedians who are good enough to perform on the show. The *Late Show* is one of the only television shows that has a booker who is also a comedian. I think it makes sense to have someone who is touring the country and performing at clubs every week to look out for talented stand-ups. The show gets a wider array of talent than shows that just review submissions or hold auditions in the city where the show tapes.

Eddie came to San Francisco when I had just started. I was probably a year or two into comedy. He worked the weekend at Cobb's Comedy Club and then held an audition showcase. Tom Sawyer, the owner of Cobb's, booked the showcase. At the time I was disappointed that I hadn't been invited. Everyone on the showcase was better than me, or at least more senior than me. And looking back now, there was no way I should have been on that showcase. But I still wanted to be. I watched the auditions, and it was awful. There was almost no crowd, and the people who were there weren't great laughers. I saw some great comics (some who have since been on *Letterman*) go up and die that night. It was ugly. Part of me was happy I wasn't on that show—happy that my first impression with the *Letterman* booker wasn't some awful show. But part of me thought I would've been the one to get that audience rolling in the aisles.

In truth I wouldn't have, but my ego believed I would have. It's that same ego that all comics have. It's what allows us to get onstage in front of strangers in the first place.

I didn't introduce myself to Eddie at the auditions that night. I figured that night belonged to those comics, not me. And I figured that Eddie and the show would eventually hear about me. They'd hear how good I was and start asking for me to audition for them. Almost five years later that hadn't happened. But with all the recent noise I'd been making, the executive producers had heard about me, and it seemed now maybe Eddie had, too.

It turns out Eddie hadn't heard about me from the *Dying to Do Letterman* campaign, but from a source I never would have guessed: Tom Sawyer. The owner of Cobb's had called Eddie about me. As strange as it was to be hearing the booker of the *Late Show* on my voicemail, it was even more surreal to hear him say, "I heard about you from Tom Sawyer, who spoke very highly of you." Tom had always given me stage time and had even given me my first paid week, but he wasn't one to hand out compliments or let people know where they stood. The only feedback you ever got from Tom was your position on his showcase list. I knew he liked what I did, but I had no idea it was enough to recommend me to Eddie Brill. I figured he must have heard about my campaign and decided to lend a hand.

Eddie went on to say he wanted to see some of my stand-up. He gave me his address at the show and requested a five-minute tape of material that I thought was good enough for the show.

Holy crap. My emotions were all over the place. I was excited. My noise had worked. Not how I had expected, but it had worked. I was grateful and touched that an unexpected acquaintance had vouched for me without any prodding. I was floored that the booker for *Letterman* had called me. I was overjoyed. I was scared. I think I might even have been aroused. Not really. But I was scared.

I was scared that the booker for *Letterman* had asked to see my comedy. I now had to put my money where my mouth was. That's not a great metaphor when you're swimming in debt. I believed I was good enough to be on the show; I had proven to audiences that I was good enough to be on the show. But none of that really mattered. The only person who mattered was the booker for the show, Eddie Brill. And he had just called me and asked for a DVD. This is what I had been working for, and it was frightening to face it. This was the moment of truth.

.I called Eddie back and got his voicemail. I doubt he was as impressed with mine as I was with his. I told him I got his message, and I'd get something together for him right away. That wasn't exactly the truth, but I didn't know that at the time.

22

The Right Tape at the Right Time

Here's a little truism about being a stand-up comic: You never have a good tape when you need it. When I say "tape," I mean DVD, or whatever format it is your set might be requested on. Almost all the work you get in comedy is the result of bookers viewing—and liking—a recording of your act. You record your sets and send them out to bookers to get more work. But when someone specifically asks for a tape, comics never have one ready.

This phenomenon first came to my attention when I was starting out in San Francisco. I was hanging out at Cobb's, and one of the top comics in the city, one of the headliners, came in and told the staff that he needed as many sets as possible that week because the people at *Late Night with Conan O'Brien* were asking to see his tape. He was obviously stressing out because he wanted to strike while the iron was hot and get them something right away.

I had seen this comic blow it up every time he took the stage. How did he not have a tape ready for just this instance? He should have a box full of tapes to choose from for just such an occasion. I didn't get it.

A short year later I understood. As my comic friends increasingly referred me to other comedy clubs and bookers, I started to get a lot of calls to "send us a tape right away." At first I sent the best tape I had, which seemed like the obvious choice. But when I didn't get booked, I started to wonder why. It turns out, the tape of me doing my best isn't always what they want.

Every booker is looking for something different, and to some extent, specific. Some want the tape to be squeaky clean. Others want to make sure you can play to a rowdy crowd. Some want to see a tape that hasn't been edited, that is completely from one show. Some want to see you performing in multiple places so they know the good set wasn't a fluke. Some bookers want to see a short five- to ten-minute set to get a feel for you and what you can do, while others want a thirty- or forty-five-minute tape. There are clubs that don't want to see you interacting with the crowd, and there are bookers who want to see that.

The only way to know what bookers want is by asking them, and then verifying the information with other comedians who have gotten work from them. Many times what bookers say they want and what they actually want is different, so it is important to check with comedians working for them. The result is never having the right tape at the right time, tailor-made for a certain booker and his or her needs at that time, unless you tape every set.

Very few comics tape every single set. For me it's so time consuming to get everything set up and stable as the crowd is filing in that it isn't worth it. I have a particular routine I do every time before I go onstage, which allows me to focus and prepare. Setting up a tripod and camera before each set would interfere with that routine. In fact, any time I have taped a set myself, I feel rushed and out of whack. I'm worrying more about the tape than I am about the set.

Now I understand why that comic didn't have a tape ready to send to *Conan*. The fact that it was a tape for a television show made it even harder to have one ready. Every late-night show is different. The tape you'd send to *Letterman* would contain very different material from the tape you'd send to *Leno* or *Kimmel*.

Plain and simple, when Eddie Brill asked for a tape, I didn't have one ready. I know it's extra silly that I had started a project to get on the show and didn't have a tape for them. Honestly, I assumed they'd ask me to audition somewhere. I had a bunch of jokes I thought would be good for the show, but I had never put them in the specific order I would want to do them. I was playing comedy clubs and doing thirty minutes to an hour, so it would have been difficult to front load my set with all the jokes I'd want to do on the show. In a long set I spaced those jokes out so they flowed naturally into each other. Short sets don't work the same way.

Okay, enough explaining, justifying, and making excuses. You get it. I didn't have a set ready. And now I needed one. Here comes another comedy truism: When you are taping your sets for something specific, you're never going to nail it. I don't know if it's the comedy gods (or demons) messing with us or what, but the minute you strive for a tape, everything goes wrong. If you've been practicing a set over and over in front of great audiences, the minute you set up a camera there will be a small crowd. Or a heckler. Or a waitress who drops a tray of drinks in the middle of your set. Or you'll mess up the jokes, or the order. Something always goes wrong. You never get the tape you need on the first try.

This was practically a moot point anyway. When Eddie called me, I had just jumped on the road for a month-long trip and hadn't brought my camera. I would be working with some comics who had cameras, so that might work. Some clubs had cameras, but they were usually awful and made a great set look average, at best. Plus, as I mentioned before, I would have to front load my set with the jokes I'd want to do and sacrifice the rest of the set. This would have me limping to the finish and leaving a bad impression on the club. I couldn't afford that.

So my strategy for those four weeks was just to figure out what jokes I wanted to do. I'd practice and tighten the bits I wanted to get on tape and then line up a short set to tape when I got back to Los Angeles. I had a few jokes I wanted to perform on *Letterman*, but as the weeks went by, I kept finding more in my repertoire that I wanted to include. By the time I got home I had over ten minutes of material I had to choose from. The sets on late-night television are five minutes. I had twice as much. Not good.

I had put a lot of time and effort into getting to this point, where Eddie Brill would request a tape. I had dedicated my adult life to comedy, created an act, sacrificed a more stable lifestyle, and more recently threw everything on the line to let the world know my dream to be on *Letterman*. And it had worked. I was in the exact spot I wanted to be. I couldn't blow it now that I was so close. I was in uncharted territory and I needed some advice. Luke Skywalker had Yoda. I needed to find my Yoda. This was so big I figured I needed a bunch of Yodas. I don't know what the plural of Yoda is—Yodi? Yoders? Yodentia? I don't know, but I needed them and their advice.

23

The Letterman List

While I was on the road that month, my friend and fellow comic Paul Morrissey sent me a list of every stand-up comic who had ever appeared on Letterman's show. I decided to send a letter to each comic on the list, asking for advice. It was an amazing list, and I still don't know where he got it. It even included the comedians from Letterman's original NBC show that followed Johnny Carson. I tried to track every one of them down to ask them if I could interview them about their experience: when they got on; how they got on; how their set went when they were on; what advice they had for someone like me who was trying to get on.

The letter I sent out basically said: My name is Steve Mazan. I'm a comedian. I have cancer. I'm trying to fulfill my dream of performing stand-up on David Letterman's show. I know you've been on there, and I'd love to interview you about your experience.

The response was surprising. Some comics whom I expected to say yes, said no—even some comics I had worked with. I was positive they'd lend a hand, but they didn't. A couple of comics agreed, but then ignored any subsequent communication. I'm sure for some of these people it was hard to say no, even though they wanted to, so they said yes and then just avoided me. I'm sure those who turned down my request or just ignored it had good reasons.

Equally surprising were the people who said yes—some of the biggest names in comedy agreed to be interviewed. TV stars like Ray Romano, Kevin Nealon, Daniel Tosh, and Jim Gaffigan. Two of my favorites, Brian Regan and Arj Barker, agreed. Even the big comedians from San Francisco who had been on the show, Will Durst and Larry "Bubbles" Brown, said yes. As a bonus, every one of them agreed to let me tape the interviews for the documentary.

The first comic I interviewed after returning home to L.A. was Nick Griffin. I had worked with Nick at the Sacramento Punch Line when I first started. His comedy is dark and biting. Comics really like him. In fact, word is he's currently Letterman's favorite comedian. When I first interviewed him in 2006, he had been on the show once. Since then I think he's been on five or six times.

Nick was extremely helpful. He told me story after story of his attempts to get on the show, and he shared his strategies. He even told me which of my jokes would be good to submit. I felt bad when we did post-production on the documentary, because we couldn't find Nick's interview. I must have lost it somewhere along the way. It's too bad because he had some great stories. Luckily, I still remember some. On top of the great interview, Nick referred me to Daniel Tosh of "Tosh.o." Tosh's career was really taking off at this point, so I was incredibly grateful to Nick for encouraging Daniel to help me.

I interviewed Daniel Tosh at the Irvine Improv before one of his shows. Denise came with me. I had never met him before, and he was friendly and funny. He asked if he could lie on the couch in the green room and hide under a blanket for the interview. He wanted it to look like I was interviewing him in his bed for the documentary. I said "Sure, why not." Daniel had made his television debut on *Letterman*, and he was very proud of that. He said he had late-night offers before that, but he wanted to make his first late-night stand-up appearance on *Letterman*. He talked at length about what *Letterman* meant to him and the prestige it held for comedians. Daniel thought Dave's show was the best, which is why he held out for it. It was cool to hear someone else talk about how much *Letterman* meant to them. Especially someone of Daniel Tosh's caliber.

Jim Gaffigan was working on the TBS comedy *My Boys* when he agreed to let me interview him. I waited for him in his trailer until he got a break from shooting. Gaffigan's love for *Letterman* was equal to mine. Like me, he identified with Dave because he was a Midwestern guy. He bonded with Letterman's humor especially in college, and at one point in the interview, while talking about his early years in comedy, Jim used these exact words: "I was dying to do *Letterman*." I could have talked to Jim about *Letterman* and comedy forever. The interview was incredibly educational. Although Gaffigan was one of the funniest people in the world, he took stand-up seriously. I really liked that.

Arj Barker was one of the big comedians in San Francisco when I started, and one of my early comedy idols. He moved to L.A soon after I arrived on the scene and started showing up everywhere on television. Arj was different and strange. Where other comics would be big and loud, Arj would be small and subtle. In Olympic gymnastics and figure skating, each performance is judged according to the difficulty of the sequence. If comedy was like that, Arj would be the quadruple axel. He attempts a type of comedy that is much more difficult than what most comics do. I interviewed Arj before his set at the Hollywood Improv. We did the interview in a small room upstairs. Arj and I were acquainted. I had worked with him in El Paso, Texas, for a few nights a couple of years earlier, but I didn't really know him well. He was good friends with my buddy Cash Levy. Arj cracked me up right away when he told me when he was on *Letterman*, and I followed up by asking him if that was the only time he had been on *Letterman*.

"Yeah." Then he paused and said, "How many times have *you* been on?"

It was classic Arj. He was also a guy who took comedy seriously. He took time to talk about the process that got him on the show. As with the other interviews, I talked to Arj for about half an hour, but could've easily done twice that.

My next road trip took me to the Punch Line in San Francisco. I brought my camera to try to get a tape of my set for Eddie Brill, but never got a good one. I did, however, get two great interviews with San Francisco comedy icons: political comedian Will Durst and Bay Area legend Larry "Bubbles" Brown.

Will does all kinds of comedy, but most of it is political. When he did political jokes on the old CBS *Letterman* show, the producers freaked because, according to them, they hadn't approved the material. Will claimed they did. Immediately following his set, he was banned from any future appearances. What a crazy story. At the end of the interview, Will joked that I should be helping him get back on *Letterman*.

When I got into comedy and mentioned to people I was a comedian, they would always ask if I knew Larry "Bubbles" Brown. Or, more accurately, if I knew "Bubbles." Larry has been in the business for three decades and still hangs out at the club like he's a newbie. His style is very whiny and self-deprecating (picture Droopy Dog doing comedy). Rumor has it, comedian Paula Poundstone gave Larry the nickname "Bubbles," an ironic declaration of his un-bubbly disposition. That, or because he was trying to talk her into a hot tub. The truth is still debated.

Of all of the comedians I interviewed, I was closest to Bubbles. Or Bubs, as I call him. We're friends who have worked together dozens of times. Still, when I interviewed him about *Letterman*, he shared stories I had never heard. The first was about how he nailed an audition in front of some CBS *Letterman* show producers who were visiting San Francisco in the mid 1980s. He said it was still one of the best sets of his life. He had been doing comedy only a couple of years, but they booked him immediately. A few months later, when he went to New York to film the show, they had him do a warm-up set the night before at a club. He died. The producers lost confidence in him and canceled his appearance. They told him to keep working and flew him home. What a terrible story.

A year later Bubbles was asked to perform on Joan Rivers' late-night show. Larry knew two things. One: *Letterman* was the show he wanted to do. Two: Joan Rivers' show wouldn't last. Bubs decided to call the *Letterman* people and let them know Joan's show wanted him. *Letterman*'s people called him back and said they wanted him, too. He did *Letterman* instead.

Weeks later, back in Los Angeles, I interviewed Kevin Nealon. He was the most playful interview I did. I met him on the set of *Weeds*. He was funny from the moment I walked into his trailer and shook his hand.

KEVIN: Hi Steve, come on in.
ME: Thanks.

KEVIN: Did anyone follow you?

ME: (confused) Huh?

KEVIN: Have a seat over there.

ME: Thanks, Kevin. I really appreciate your taking the time to do this.

KEVIN: No problem. Been a big fan of you my entire life.

He was funny. But just like the other comics, Kevin took comedy seriously, and he had some great advice and incredible stories about his *Letterman* experience. He told one story about having to completely scrap his planned *Letterman* set the day of the show and do a different set. Since he had no club where he could practice it, he performed it for the maid at his hotel. He didn't think she even understood English.

For most of the interviews neither Joke nor Biagio were available to shoot, so a great cameraman and friend Adam Sampson filled in. But for the Nealon interview, both Joke and Biagio were available. After the interview, I thanked Kevin, and Biagio asked if he could remain inside the trailer so he could shoot Kevin Nealon showing me out. So Kevin showed me to the door and opened it. I walked out and he said good-bye and to make sure to let him know if I get on *Letterman*. Then he closed the door and said directly to the camera, "It's never gonna happen."

I was outside, so I had no idea. Biagio showed me the footage later. He prepped me by warning me not to get mad. How could I get mad? It was just as playful as he was in the rest of the interview. It was hilarious. I expected nothing less from Nealon.

Brian Regan was, and is, my favorite comedian. If you ask 100 comedians who their favorite comic is, I bet most of them say Brian Regan. He's the top guy. He's gotten so big that he only plays theaters now. The amazing thing is that he got to that level by just doing stand-up comedy. Most comics get to that level by doing something other than stand-up, like sitcoms or movies. But Brian made his name by being a great comedian. I can't think of another comic who has done that.

Brian let me interview him when he was in Los Angeles for some work. He invited me up to his hotel room. He was casual and friendly. I had met him once briefly at Cobb's Comedy Club when he was performing there. It was packed, and I watched both his shows while standing in the hallway that lead to the bar.

One big problem with Brian's interview: we couldn't use half the footage because Brian was so funny that he cracked up Joke and Biagio so much that they couldn't hold the camera still. By this point, he had been on the *Late Show* seventeen times. I think he's appeared over twenty times now. I couldn't believe I was getting advice and hearing *Letterman* stories from the greatest comic alive. I was nervous, starstruck, and excited all at once. But I told myself to calm down because I was here to get advice, not fawn over Brian. By the time I was done interviewing him, I realized that the documentary was allowing me to compile some incredible footage of great comedians talking about their process and comedy. It was pretty cool.

Brian's manager, Rory Rosegarten, had set up the interview. He also set up a meeting with the most famous comic I interviewed—Ray Romano. It would be hard to interview anyone, comic or not, more famous. This was maybe a year after *Everybody Loves Raymond* went off the air. You'd never know he was one of the richest, most famous people in Hollywood. He was down-to-earth and unassuming.

Ray has probably the most famous *Letterman* story ever. It was a hot day in the summer of '95 when he appeared on *Letterman*. Dave was doing a goofy bit where they cut people's pants off at the knee. Dave called it "summer-izing" people's pants. They did it to several people on the street, a couple in the audience, and then Dave did it to himself. I think they even did it to the first guest, Mel Gibson. One segment before Ray was supposed to make his debut on the show, a producer ran in and said they had to cut his pants. The producer said it would be funny if Ray walked out like that.

Ray had to make an important decision immediately. Cut his pants or not. He knew the audience would laugh if he walked out like that. But he also knew it would affect the rest of his set. Mel Gibson was a frequent guest and a big star; he earned the right to be one of the guys and cut his pants. Ray was new and worried that doing it would set a precedent of familiarity that would change the way his set would be received. On the other hand, maybe Dave would be mad if he refused. He had no way of knowing. In the end he decided not to cut his pants. Ray figured he should go on the show the way he had planned and practiced; that way he wouldn't second-guess a last-minute change. He had a great set. A few weeks later *Letterman*'s production company called and said that Dave was interested in doing a sitcom around Ray. Who knows how it might have gone had he decided to cut his pants?

Besides great stories, Ray had some great suggestions, like just worry about being funny and trust that everything else would fall into place. Although in the end, he admitted it made him uncomfortable to think I might take his advice. He joked that he didn't want the weight of knowing his guidance might make or break my dream.

I learned a lot from interviewing all those great comics. Although each path to *Letterman* was different, all the comics had two similar beliefs. One, they all think the *Late Show with David Letterman* is the pinnacle of televised stand-up comedy and that an appearance would be hard to achieve. Number two, when it comes to picking material to submit for the show, don't overthink it. Every one of them advised that all any aspiring comic could do was send the show the best example of what he or she does, and hope that it's a fit.

Brian Regan summed it up best: "I feel like as an artist you should do what you wanna do, what you think is funny. And hopefully other people think it's funny as well, including the *Letterman* show. Hopefully they go 'Yeah, man, this is what we want.' But I think the moment you start to go, 'What do they want?' I truly believe that's a line where you start making a mistake."

Spoken like a true Yoda.

24

Forget the Cutting-Room Floor

A ll right, I had the best advice from the best in the business, guidance from the greatest comics who had performed exactly where I wanted to perform. The overwhelming consensus was to submit the jokes I thought best represented me and my act. It was time to figure out which bits those were, get them on tape, and get that tape to Eddie Brill.

I had to take the ten minutes of jokes I thought were good enough for the show and cut it down to five. I couldn't do it. It was so hard. When I narrowed down my act to the best ten minutes, it was relatively easy to cut more suggestive jokes and bits that required me to interact with the crowd. But now I had to choose the best five minutes out of that. It was difficult to choose one joke over another. They were all All-Stars at this point. I didn't want to cut any of them. When I put any of them on the chopping block, I second-guessed my decision right away. I needed more help.

Lee and Gary came over. I appreciated their input, but it was also difficult for them to suggest which jokes should be cut. These jokes were like my babies. I loved them all equally. To make matters worse, Lee and Gary disagreed on a few of them. Even when we all agreed on axing one, we ended up putting it back because it flowed well or lead nicely into another that we were keeping. I can't remember if it was Gary or Lee, but one of them suggested just sending a ten-minute tape.

Eddie wanted a five-minute tape. But the more we all thought about it, the more it made sense. I had made a bunch of noise over at the show. Eddie had heard about me from a respected person in the business. He asked me for the tape. Chances were with all this attention he might watch more than the usual five minutes he requested.

And . . . I had cancer. I was asking to be looked at because my time might be short. If he was willing to look at one five-minute set, why wouldn't he watch a little more in this special case? If he watched five minutes and didn't like it, wouldn't the fact that all those people had sent e-mails recommending me, that Tom Sawyer had said I was good, that time was of the essence for me, push him to maybe watch the rest of it? Lee, Gary, and I thought so. If Eddie didn't like someone's five minutes, he probably told them they weren't right for the show or said to send another tape when they had five new minutes. Rather than waste time, why not send the entire ten minutes now?

It was a gamble, but one worth taking. Gary had a show coming up at the Ontario Improv, which he could probably get me on for ten minutes. Great. I'd bring my camera and we'd try to get it all on tape.

I was excited but not too confident. This was officially the first time I knew exactly what I wanted to get on tape, and as I explained before, I was aware that you never get a tape when you need it.

This time I was wrong. The comedy demons took the day off and we got a good tape. The club was packed and the crowd that night was great, which was lucky because the show was in the middle of the week. Gary hosted and blew it up. I was actually a little nervous following him. Gary is a great comic who does a lot of "crowd work." Rather than do prepared material, he gets up there and messes with the crowd. He's really good at it. Sometimes Gary's so good at it that the next comic up struggles. The crowd is so impressed with an impromptu comic that someone with prepared material pales in comparison. So when the crowd went nuts for Gary, I was both encouraged and worried.

I got all my jokes out, in the correct order, and they all did well. As Gary came back onstage to take the mic from me, he smiled and whispered, "You got it, Buddy."

Could I really have it? I needed this tape as much as any comic has ever needed a tape before. What are the odds I'd get it on first try?

I had felt a little nervous and hoped it didn't show up on the tape, so Gary suggested we watch it right away when we got home.

The sound was perfect. You could hear me clearly and could tell the audience loved it, but I looked tense and not as loose as I normally am. Gary said he couldn't tell and was positive Eddie wouldn't notice. That was good enough for me. We shook hands on a job well done, and I dropped the DVD in the mail the next morning.

Here is the set list and jokes featured on my ten-minute tape to Eddie:

Wake Up

Everyone is so nice here. [Smiling] I appreciate that.
Have you noticed in general people are not as nice as they used to be? Some people are actually afraid of people they

haven't met yet. I'll give ya an example of what I'm talking about. A couple years ago I met this woman out at a bar, we talked all night, flirted a little bit, and at the end of the night I asked her if I could give her a ride home. She said "No, we just met." [act out her shaking head wildly no] I said, "We've been talking for, like, four hours. What are you worried about?" [She shakes her head wildly no again and speaks in shrilly voice] She says, "I don't want to wake up in a ditch somewhere." . . . What? I'm like, "Don't be silly . . . you're not gonna wake up."

Best Thing

She thought that was funny, too, and we've been married ever since. And I'm not just saying this, but in all honesty this woman may be the best thing that has ever happened to me . . . no, don't clap or "awwww"—she's not that great, I've just had an awful life.

5/3

I haven't had an awful life. Awful year. I started it by getting arrested . . . Okay, too soon for that story? We'll come back to the getting arrested portion of my act. . . . My car insurance went up this year, too. But I saw an advertisement last week on TV for a company that said they could insure me for a fraction of what I've been paying. . . . Unfortunately, that fraction was 5/3 [five-thirds]

Insurance

I'm always worried about my insurance. You ever go out with some friends and someone gets too drunk and you have to drive them home? But they have their car, so you have to drive them home in their own car? I'm always worried that insurance doesn't cover me on their car. My friends always say the same stupid thing [act drunk], "Don't worry, Dude. Take my keys. Anything happens we'll just switch places." What? We're gonna switch places? That's gonna solve everything? Ten minutes later we're in a terrible mangled accident. [act mangled, arm in precarious position behind head, then slowly turn towards passenger] "Dude, come on switch places . . . hurry up, before the cops get here. Come on switch. . . . Dude, stop messing around. . . . Dude! [react to his unresponsiveness—Dead?] Dude? . . . Oh no [spot something in distance] "Fireman! Fireman, switch us. He's dead but I don't have insurance . . . hurry up . . . oh no, here come the cops. . . . just roll me on top of him . . . let them figure out what was going on."

Towels

I stay at a lot of hotels, and five years ago none of them were doing this but now they all have a "Clean Towel Policy." It's always a placard hanging on the bathroom door or a little tent on the sink. And it's very dramatic. It's always like, [soft voice] "Welcome. We're trying to save the world. If you could help out by re-using your towel that'd be great." . . . Or . . . "If you're a lazy jerk, you could just kick it under the sink and our maid will get it on the morning. Then when you wake up, Shamu will be floating at the top of his tank. Because you don't care about the environment, do you?"

It's the most overbearing thing just to get you to re-use your towel. And let's be honest, they're not doing it to save the world, they're doing it to save their cleaning lady a few loads of laundry. The best one I've ever seen was a couple weeks ago. It was hanging on the doorknob, and instead of a white placard it was multicolored like an aquarium. And it had their message, "Hang it up if you'll use it again, put it on floor and we'll get you a new one." But above the message was a circle. And in the circle there was a dolphin. But not a whole dolphin, just his head. And he was smiling. *[Act out smiling dolphin head]*. So what this hotel was trying to insinuate by putting his head on top of the message was that HE was the one who said this. Like it was HIS clean-towel policy. Like there had been a porpoise press conference where he came out and made a speech *[Act out dolphin clicking message and using fin to kick towel under sink]*.

Ya know what? I'll help out with your stupid policy, just be honest about it. You're not doing it for the dolphin. In that circle should be the poor, illegal immigrant cleaning lady. *[act out cleaning lady in circle with hands up]* "Okay, I've been here since six AM, making minimum wage . . . cleaning up your beer bottles and condom wrappers . . . and whatever that blue stuff was on your pillow . . . I have no guess on that one. But I'd like to go home sometime. . . . Let's be honest with each other. At home you don't wash that bath towel but every three weeks!"

Wink

Times have changed. When I was a kid, my dad used to take me to the bar with him. . . . I know now it was a bad idea, but when I was a kid I loved it. He'd take me to the bar and the guys hanging out with him would be totally cool to me.

They'd pat me on the back, flip me a quarter, and say, "Here ya go, kid, go play some pinball." And when they patted me on the back, they gave me a little wink. And that wink made me feel like I was one of the guys. One of the men. I felt good. And I always thought, "When I grow up, I'm gonna be that kind of guy. The kind that winks at a kid and makes him feel good about himself. . . ." [shake head slowly no] Times have changed! That doesn't make kids feel good about themselves . . . it makes them tell their parents . . . and sometimes a jury . . . and you can never explain that away, "No listen, it's a mistake. Look he was just a cute kid and—NO. NO, NOT CUTE! . . . He was a nice kid, and I was going to give him a quarter for—FOR NOTHING! . . . For nothing. Look it's gonna make sense. Listen. Men used to do it to me when I was a kid—WAIT, WAIT, that's coming out wrong . . . so it makes me realize times HAVE changed. Either that, or my dad's friends were hitting on me.

Standing "O"

Please, when I finish, no standing ovation. You think as a performer I'd love the standing ovation, but I don't. Because I'm in the audience a lot when it breaks out and it's always awkward. You're sitting there enjoying yourself, you're clapping [act out], and then you look around and see people getting up . . . and you're like, "We're standing? For this guy? All right." It's just peer pressure, isn't it? Are you ever the first person standing? No! We all hate that guy. [act out] "Thanks a lot, Jerko. I paid to sit down, not stand. I think I pulled something." Listen, if someone is obviously deserving, then okay. Someone cures cancer? Standing ovation . . . Mother

*Teresa? Standing ovation . . . well, that's a bad example,
she's dead . . . well, if she shows up, then definitely standing
ovation! [act out] "Oh my god! Thanks for coming, we didn't
expect you. Thanks for the second coming, this is great."*

*Ya know it's hard to think of people who deserve that even
when they were alive. Like my hero growing up, Rosa Parks.
I saw her three or four times at college lecture halls talking
about her incredibly heroic life. People would always want
to give her a standing ovation. . . . Bad idea. I stood for her
and BOOM! She was in my seat. [act out Rosa sitting and not
giving up seat] Thankfully you all knew who I was talking
about. I told that joke at some club last week and they had
no sense of American history. One guy was like, "Who the
hell is Rosa Parks? . . . Is that that Mexican valet service?"*

Test

*I'm getting older and have to start worrying about certain
health concerns. One of those for men is testicular cancer.
Good news. I got checked up and everything came out clean.
BUT then the doctor gave me a take-home test to do on my
own every six months. Men, you'd better be ready; it says
some strange things on there. Like #1 [act out reading card]
"Check for lumps." [look down] Okay, one, two . . . Check. All
present and accounted for . . . #2 "Check for discoloration."
Okay, I'm gonna be honest here. I'm not sure what color they
are supposed to be . . . Is there a Home Depot color swatch
test I can use? [act out flipping through swatches and
comparing] No. No. No. Ahhhh. [look at matching swatch]
Hmmm, Salmon Suede . . . who knew? But here's the thing:
it's easy to check yourself up on top, it's much harder to*

examine yourself back up underneath. If I could bend over that far, cancer wouldn't be my problem. . . . So what I'm saying is, the only way to examine yourself back up underneath is if you can find, like, a tilted floor level mirror . . . long story short, THAT is how I got arrested at Footlocker.

Thank you, Good-night.

25

Anticipation

I believe it was the great American poet Thomas Petty who said, "The waiting is the hardest part." It's true. I sent that first DVD to Eddie Brill on August 18, 2006. Two weeks later, I still had not heard anything.

Maybe Eddie was mad that I had taken so long to get him the tape. I'm sure he knew I couldn't just send any tape I had laying around. He was a comic; he had to understand it took time to get the exact tape. At least I hoped he understood.

With each day that went by, I was less sure. I was so anxious to hear some news. I figured there were three possibilities. One, he got the DVD but hadn't had time to look at it yet. Two, he never received it. Three, he got it and thought it was so bad that I didn't even deserve a call.

I tried to keep busy at home. But that was frustrating because part of chasing this dream was to help me to not focus on all the bills and health problems. I did every comedy show I was offered, paid or not, just so I could keep busy. I wasn't very fun to live with those weeks. Actually, I was probably in a good mood for the first week because I had a sense of accomplishment and eagerness.

That eagerness gave way to nervousness after a week. The week after that, it was full-blown anxiety. I was short-tempered and fidgety. Every e-mail and phone call was a disappointment. Because it wasn't from Eddie. It was all I could think about.

Denise was great. But I was mad at her for being so great. That's how ridiculous I was being. Finally, after a month I gave up. He must have hated the DVD. I sent him an e-mail asking if he had received it. He didn't respond. Maybe my e-mails were getting lost. I resolved to move forward as if he hated that DVD. I began working on new jokes to send him.

Of course, then he called.

I came out of the bathroom one day in mid-September and saw I had missed a call. I didn't recognize the 917 area code. That got me excited. I opened my computer to check the location. While I was looking it up, my phone beeped, indicating I had a voice-mail. My stomach tightened. At the same time the search result showed 917 was a New York area code. Jackpot! Here we go.

I set up the camera, started recording, sat back on the couch and took a deep breath. I hit play on the voicemail. "Hi, Steve. This is Eddie Brill. How you doing, sir? . . . It's Tuesday afternoon here in New York. I watched your DVD . . . and I have some, uh . . . words for you." Then he left his number and finished with, "All right, hope all is well, and I'll talk to you soon."

What the hell just happened? I was in shock. I couldn't move. My body was paralyzed except for my stomach, which felt like it was fighting its way to the floor. Did he actually say, "I have some, uh . . . words for you?"

I hit PLAY on the message and listened again. Yep. He said that. Words for me? That did not sound good. It sounded like something out of an old movie. Anytime I heard anyone say that, they were about to get into a fight. "Hey, Buddy, I've got some words for you!" PUNCH!

My DVD couldn't have been that bad. Could it? There was only one way to find out. Call him back. I got a drink of water and took another deep breath. I hit DIAL on the missed call number. It started to ring. It kept ringing. After about seven rings it rolled to voicemail. I left Eddie a message telling him I got his message and that I'd be available the rest of the day.

Eddie called back half an hour later. But I was in the bathroom again. Damn that stupid spicy lemonade cleanse! I had my phone with me in the bathroom and couldn't afford missing him again, so I answered it. I wasn't going to miss this chance.

Eddie was nice. He didn't want to punch me. He didn't want to put me on the *Late Show*, either. Eddie said he thought I was a really funny comic. But that wasn't enough to get on the show. As an example Eddie told me his favorite comic was Robert Schimmel, but Robert would probably never be on the show because his act just wasn't the right fit. He said I was good, but the jokes on this DVD were not right for the show. He said, "Let's go through them."

Honestly, I didn't really want to. I was so disappointed. I had sent in what I thought was my best and it wasn't good enough. I thought those jokes were right for the show. I didn't want to hear in detail why they were so wrong. Not right then, at least. But I didn't have a choice. Eddie's a busy guy. If I was going to learn why they weren't right, this was the chance—the chance to hone my craft and find jokes that were right for the show. I picked up a pen, tried to sound positive, and said, "Okay."

Eddie liked the "Wake up" joke. His only problem was that it seemed harsh to open with. He thought it took away from my likability. He didn't mention the "my wife is the best thing that ever happened to me" bit. He skipped right over it.

"I really like this five-thirds bit. I laughed out loud . . . and Dave would love that joke."

Okay. He liked and was complimentary about two of the first three jokes. What was the problem?

The rest of the set was the problem.

When he got to the driving a drunk friend home bit, I started taking a few tough shots. He said that bit was way too physical for the show. They were looking for jokes that were well written and didn't have to be acted out so much. This one really hurt because when I wrote it a year and a half earlier, I was convinced it would be the bit that got me on the show. People loved that bit. Eddie didn't.

The hotel towels joke he really liked, too. Or at least part of it. Eddie liked the dolphin making the policy, but said that the part about the immigrant cleaning lady was mean.

He didn't care for the wink joke. He said it dealt with children being looked at as sex objects, a topic that would not make it on the show. This was my personal favorite joke at the time, so it hurt to know it had no chance.

Other comics often pick my standing ovation bit as their favorite from my act. So I thought Eddie would like it, too. Nope. He thought it was mean, too. And he said the Rosa Parks part was "cheap." Ouch. I was up against the ropes now.

I wanted to throw in the towel, but there was one more round. The cancer exam joke. Eddie didn't like it at all. He said it was way too dirty for television. Then he added, "I thought with your condition, maybe you'd have something a little more personal and meaningful on the cancer angle." Down for the count.

Eddie finished by reiterating that he thought I was good, but I needed to work on a few things. He said I talked too fast and I looked nervous (I knew it!). My delivery was monotone and my jokes were a little too mean. He said to stop asking so many rhetorical questions. He suggested avoiding jokes that relied on characters, physical humor, or telling long stories. Last, Eddie said he'd be happy to look at anything I wanted to send him in the future.

I felt like I had been beaten to a pulp. I muscled out a thank-you and said good-bye.

I hung up and sat stunned on the couch for over an hour. My campaign had led me right where I wanted to be. I had given him my best stuff. And it wasn't anywhere close to good enough. I was too shocked to cry or yell. I was numb.

26

What Are Friends For?

Well, if there was a bright side to talking with Eddie, it was that I didn't feel anxious anymore. Now I just felt awful. I felt like the past seven years of my life had been a waste. I was convinced that my act and I were good enough for the show, and now the only person who mattered had told me just the opposite.

I lay in bed for a couple days. Denise was great as usual. She saw all the positives in what Eddie said. She said I was good enough; I just had to find the right material to show him. It didn't make me feel better. Only one thing was going to make me feel better: commiserating with my best friends.

Lee and I met Gary at his apartment. They wanted to hear all about the call with Eddie. I laid it all out for them, from the missed calls in the bathroom to the final rundown of what I needed to work on. They were great friends. They stuck up for every one of my jokes and disagreed with most of Eddie's points. They had seen much meaner and dirtier material on TV, even on the *Late Show* itself.

Lee cited Ray Romano's stand-up set that got him *Everybody Loves Raymond*. On *Letterman,* Ray did a bit about being in the shower and masturbating to all the women he had met that day. We all agreed that was much more suggestive than my "wink" or "cancer exam" jokes.

Gary and Lee thought my material and I were as good as some of the other comics they had seen on the show. I don't know if they really believed that, but I believed them. And at that point all that mattered was being convinced I was good enough to be on the show so I could pick myself up and start proving it.

27

Next

Lee and Gary helped me over the next couple of weeks. I dug out every notebook I had kept since starting comedy. I ran every joke I had ever written past them. They let me know if they thought it was, or could be, good enough for my next DVD. I'm sure they were sick of hearing it all, but they didn't show it.

Gary was a "Yeah-I-think-that's-good-enough" or "Nah" judge. Lee's critiques were more in depth. His comedy was a lot more like mine, so he could see if there was something in a joke that could be salvaged.

The further I got from Eddie's call, the less it stung. I hoped he would love the new five minutes I was putting together for him and then book me, but that was a long shot at best. Somewhere in the back of my mind I knew that getting on the show would be a process. I hadn't admitted that to myself until then. And thanks to Eddie, that process was underway. I knew what I had to do now; I knew what I had to work on. Thanks to Eddie Brill I had some direction. A few months ago all I had was "impossible."

My dream had hit a roadblock, but while I was busy getting it back on track, one of Denise's dreams was coming true. She had found a vacant space in a strip mall only a few blocks from our house. After years of dreaming and weeks of negotiations with the landlord, she was going to finally open her yoga and dance studio.

Denise took me to the storefront to show me. The corner space had a lot of windows. It was locked up, but I looked through the windows and saw that it had one giant room with a little storage room in the back. Denise pointed out all the things she wanted to do with it. It warmed my heart to see her so excited.

As supportive as Denise had always been about my comedy career and my dream to get on *Letterman*, she sometimes resented it. It's hard working a job you don't love every day while your partner is doing exactly what he wants to. On top of that, my hours with comedy require me to work late into the night, which means I sleep in. Getting up early for her long commute had to be even more biting when Denise saw me lying in bed. I hoped her opening her own business would remedy this.

The night Denise signed the lease and got the keys to the space, we decided to film the first official steps into her studio. Lee ran the camera. It was dark when we got there, so we pulled our car up to the backdoor and shined the headlights. Since we had just finished a cleanse, we bought a bottle of carbonated apple juice and toasted the success of the studio.

The next month passed in a whirlwind. I spent my evenings writing jokes and practicing old ones that I wanted to get ready for my next DVD to Eddie. During the day I ran errands for Denise, who had put in her two weeks' notice at her job. If she got home early, we'd meet at her studio and work together. We had lots of painting, lighting, and cleaning to do to get it ready for classes. She named it Your Neighborhood Studio because she wanted people to feel at home there. She made the place feel welcoming.

We were in a nerve-racking frenzy trying to get everything completed the night before she was scheduled to open. Just hours before the first class was to begin, she finished the installation of the new wood floors.

But she made it. Denise had reached her dream. She opened her own studio. As terrible as the cancer diagnosis had been for us, it had also been our wake-up call. We were chasing our dreams now, not waiting for them.

Within a week of Denise's opening, I hit the road for comedy. But not just any road. This road led to the Middle East. I was going to Iraq with a group of comedians called Comics on Duty. I had been to Iraq and Afghanistan four times before to entertain the troops. From my time in the Navy I knew how boring it is to be away from your friends and family and not have any real entertainment available. I was honored to go and perform for them each and every time.

Honestly, there was a little selfishness for my trips to the Middle East. My first trip in 2003 had been completely for the troops, but it had been so rewarding that I decided to go back every chance I got. The truth about comedy clubs is that they are not in business to showcase comedy. They are in business to sell alcohol and food. Comedy is how they get people into their businesses. Once the customers are there, it's all about selling the menu. It's like a theme park. They don't make money on the attractions; they make it on the soda and snacks.

But performing for the troops was the purest form of comedy I had ever done. These soldiers needed a laugh more than anyone in the world. We performed to make them laugh. Period. I've heard people say that laughter cures. I don't know for sure, but I hope it does. What I do know is that laughter helps us forget. Maybe not forever, but at least for the amount of time we're laughing. We forget where we are. We forget what's bothering us. We forget, and there is a lot of value in that. It makes comedy noble. It makes it valuable. By making the troops laugh and forget where they are, at least for a while, we're doing something far more special than selling nachos.

This trip ended up being very different from my previous tours in Iraq. It was a lot scarier. One night after our comedy show at Camp Falcon, insurgents fired a mortar onto the base and it landed on the base's ammo dump. The result was the biggest explosions I had ever seen outside of a movie. We felt the shock of the explosions as we ran for the bunkers, which were only a few hundred yards from us. Amazingly, my friend and fellow comic Drake Witham kept the camera rolling for the biggest explosion. Needless to say, we were frightened.

In the end, the soldiers got us comics and everyone else as far away as possible until the explosions stopped. They went on for almost twelve hours! Thankfully no one was hurt. But we were somewhat traumatized. It took a couple days and several shows to shake off the ordeal and the nervousness that it might happen again at any moment. But the men and women over there are so confident and treat everything with such routine that we finally followed suit and got back to normal. Mostly.

I didn't tell Denise about the close call until we got home. She'd just worry. No reason for two of us to be nervous.

28

Dying to Do Ferguson?

In some strange way, I had accepted that cancer would do me in. I was going to fight it every step of the way and beat all the timetables, but I still somehow believed it was going to be the disease that ended my life. Being in Iraq, particularly close enough to an explosion that required us to duck shrapnel, made me realize something: I could die from any number of things. And because I truly had no idea when and how, I needed to go full throttle toward my dream.

As soon as I got back from Iraq, I got into the clubs to get my new jokes on DVD. This time it took longer to get the perfect set recorded. By the time I got the DVD, it was late December, almost four months from when I spoke with Eddie. I dropped the DVD in the mail and waited. Because it was around the holidays and the show wasn't taping, I didn't expect a quick response. And I didn't get one.

Pretty soon it was mid-January. It had been one year since I started the project. My deadline had expired, and I had failed in getting on *Letterman*. I had made progress. I had made more progress this year than I had in the other six years of my comedy career combined. I hadn't been successful with my first goal. But I could be with the next one. So I decided to give myself an extension. One more year to get on *Letterman*.

I wasn't overly disappointed about not making it in that first year. I was in the game now. I was in the process of getting on. That was big in itself. After talking with all the great comics about their *Letterman* experiences, it had been silly of me to think I could make it happen within a year. To go from the show never having heard of me to being on the show within twelve months was a longshot at best. Ray Romano said it took him a decade. Brian Regan said he auditioned several times over the years. It was naïve to expect that I would make it happen so quickly.

Even if the show had loved me and everything I was doing, it would take time to get in the rotation of comics they had already scheduled for the show. I wasn't the only comedian Eddie was looking at; he had thousands of comedians to consider. Kevin Nealon told me that he found it hard to get booked on the show even after all of his success. So I didn't feel too bad for not making it that first year.

Plus, it wasn't like good things weren't happening. Being out so much and working on a set for late-night television was getting me noticed.

In December when I had been working on my second DVD for Eddie, I went to a show in Santa Monica with Cash Levy. Our mutual friend Scott Channon runs a weekend show in a little theater there. Although they get great crowds, it's not the kind of place I would tape my set for a DVD. I needed an actual comedy club for that. But Cash asked me to come out that night to watch him run through a set he was going to perform on Craig Ferguson's show the following week.

When we got there Scott said he could probably give me five minutes if I wanted it. I jumped at the chance. I'm a stage whore. I'll take stage time anywhere. Especially since I was still trying to get the perfect set for Eddie. I figured this five minutes would be good practice.

I ended up going on a few comics before Cash. I had a really good set. The crowd had been a little unresponsive before I went up, but I really got them going. It gave me confidence in this new set for Eddie. Cash went up a little later and had a great set. His set for Ferguson was tight and ready to go.

Later that evening, Cash and I stood in front of the theater to discuss the show. While we were there, another comic who was on the show came up and introduced himself as Matt Baetz. He had seen my set and thought it was really funny. After I thanked him, he mentioned that he worked on Craig Ferguson's television show.

We talked a little about the *Ferguson* show and what Matt did for them. Cash asked him if he had any tips for prepping for the show. Matt shared a couple of stories about what some other comedians had gone through and what to be ready for. I was getting excited for Cash. It was only a couple of days away.

Cash and I had to hit the road so we said good-bye to Matt. I gave him my business card, which had a PEZ dispenser with my head on it. Next to it, the slogan read, DISPENSING JOKES IN MOSTLY GOOD TASTE." Matt laughed at it. As we were about to walk away, Matt said, "Hey, Steve. You were really funny. If you have a tape, I'd be happy to pass it on to our booker."

The next day Matt and I e-mailed back and forth. I dropped a DVD in the mail of some jokes that I loved but didn't fit Eddie's criteria for *Letterman*.

At the end of January, soon after I had extended my *Letterman* deadline, I got a call from Celia Joseph, the booker for *The Late Late Show with Craig Ferguson*. She had received my DVD and wanted to know if I was available to do the show the following month. I didn't even bother opening my calendar. "Yes. I'm available."

I immediately called Denise at her studio. She answered like she always does when she's swamped. "I'm really busy checking in a class; I'll call you right back." Then she hung up. She did this all the time, so I didn't take it personally. But I had so much excitement that I didn't want to just sit and wait for her to call back. I got on my bike and rode as fast as I could the couple of blocks to her studio.

"I'm gonna be on the Craig Ferguson show!"

Denise's eyes got wide. "Oh my God! Are you serious?" As I nodded yes, she jumped up and ran to me and gave me a huge hug. We had a celebratory dinner that night when she got home. It was a "'last hurrah" anyway, because the following week we were due to start the Master Cleanse again. After our dinner we called my mom and tell her the good news. It was almost eleven in Chicago, but luckily my mom is a night owl. She picked up the phone on the second ring.

"Mom, I have some good news."

"What?"

"I'm gonna be on *The Late Late Show with Craig Ferguson!*"

Pause.

"You?" she asked.

Denise and I cracked up. We were slapping the couch at how funny a response that was. "Yes, me! Thank God you aren't booking the show!"

Next we called my dad. This one would be weird. He is a pretty sentimental guy, but he can also be a jerk for no reason sometimes, a la my wedding day. I say no reason, but the reason is probably alcohol. As I was dialing I wished it was a month later, because he gives up drinking for Lent every year. Of course, then he might be grumpy that he couldn't have a beer. I just hoped he'd be in a good mood. It took him about twenty rings to pick up. He doesn't have an answering machine because "I hate those goddamn things."

"What's up, Kiddo?" "Kiddo" was a sign he was in a good mood.

"I'm here with Denise. We have some good news to share with you."

"Denise is knocked up?"

"Nope. I'm gonna perform comedy on *The Late Late Show with Craig Ferguson*."

Pause.

"Is that the Scottish guy?"

"Yeah, Dad. The Scottish guy."

"I've only seen him a couple times. Barb and I usually watch *MASH* reruns when he's on."

I laughed. "I hope you'll watch him the night I'm on."

"Of course. How did you find out? When are you on?"

I relayed the story and gave him all the details. When I thought we were about to wrap up he said, "So are you gonna change the name of your project to Dying to Do Ferguson?

I told him no, because it was still my ultimate dream to be on *Letterman*. That was a mistake. My dad was a Jay Leno fan, and I had just opened the conversation to his dissertation on why Leno was better. He jumped on it.

"I still don't know why ya wanna be on that asshole's show.

Everyone I know likes Leno better. And that Paul Schaeffer . . . don't get me started . . ."

When my dad says, "Don't get me started," it means "I'm started."

He went on making awful remarks about Dave, the show, the band, and telling me how stupid I was to want to do that show over *Leno*. He said he just didn't get it. I knew that without his telling me.

I had tried to help him get it in the past, and I didn't want to take another swing at it now. I was in too good a mood. I told him I had to call my sister in Japan. That got him started on wondering why my sister had moved her family to Japan, and accused it of being a third world country that wasn't safe for anyone. I told him to watch the show and we'd talk soon.

Instead, I called my brother next, but he was asleep. I left him a message telling him the news. He called back the next day and was really happy for me. As a musician he, more than anyone else, knew the value of getting on these shows.

I called my sister while it was early in the day in Japan. Cathy picked up quickly. Denise and I told her the news. Of course, she was excited. We'd always joked that she would be my manager, so she said that now maybe she'd make some money. I reminded her that the show was on 12:30 AM and that the comics were on closer to 1:30 so not to count on instant fame. Japan doesn't get the show, but some American friends of hers there had a device that would record shows at their house in America and send it to their cable box in Japan.

I wanted to have a nice suit for my debut, but Denise and I couldn't afford it. Instead I wore jeans and my wedding-day burgundy blazer with a black T-shirt underneath. I spent the next two-and-a-half weeks fasting and practicing. I was able to run through the set multiple times a night in front of real crowds. By the time the tape day came around I was confident.

A town car picked up Denise, Gary, and me and took us to the studio. I was thrilled knowing I was about to make my television debut. As ready as I was, I felt nervous. When we drove through the gates at CBS television city and the driver told the guard that I was performing on the *Craig Ferguson* show, it felt real for the first time.

Celia, the booker, met us and showed us to my dressing room. They even had my name on the door. The show would be starting soon and Celia explained that another comic and I would tape at the end of the show.

Unlike other late-night shows, *Ferguson* doesn't tape everything in order, or all in the same show in which the segment will appear. Although they were taping my set in front of today's audience, they didn't know if it would be part of the rest of the show they were doing. They might hold it and include it in another show to fill a segment. So I was taping today but really didn't know when it would air.

I had at least an hour's wait till I went on. I didn't want to get more nervous, so I started walking around. I ran into the other comic, introduced myself, and wished him luck. Then I noticed that the dressing room across from mine had the actor Dylan McDermott's name on the door. I was going to go over and introduce myself. Denise liked him on *The Practice* so I thought it'd be cool for her to meet him. She didn't want me to bother him and worried I might get in trouble. I was a guest, too. Why shouldn't I be able to introduce myself and wish him luck in his interview? Denise talked me out of it.

We watched the show from the green room. I ran through the set a couple more times. I got rid of a lot of nervous energy by jumping up and down and shadowboxing, which is my usual routine before going onstage.

Once the show finished its normal taping, Craig "fake introduced" me and the other comedian to the audience and left the stage, passing my dressing room. I was confused. Wasn't he going to introduce me when I went out there? Celia came by my room and I asked her about it.

"No. Craig won't be out there while you perform. The stage manager will bring you out. We will edit in Craig's introduction later."

I was a little disappointed. Craig, like Letterman, was a comedian himself, and some of the prestige came from performing in front of them; making them laugh. Celia asked if I wanted to meet him. Of course I did. As he passed my dressing room he wished me good luck and thanked me for being there.

By this time the stage manager was introducing the other comedian. In five minutes that would be me. I went to the bathroom one more time and made sure I didn't drip on myself. How embarrassing would that be for a TV debut? I shadowboxed a little more, and then Celia and Matt Baetz came to my room and said it was time.

Denise sat in the audience with Gary. She promised they would laugh even if no one else did. The stage manager introduced me, and I took the stage. It felt really strange. The audience was decent-sized, and they had a great energy. But the cameras separated me from them. I had difficulty making eye contact with most of the crowd. Some people weren't even watching me; they were watching the TV monitors in the studio. It was so different from stand-up at a club. This explained why so many great comics come across awkward on television.

I decided to split my time looking right into the camera and pretending to scan the crowd I couldn't really see. It seemed to work. They laughed at all the right places. The crowd even reacted to subtle things, so it must be going well. The five minutes flew by. The stage manager was counting down the final minute with some cue cards. Telling me when I had forty-five, thirty, fifteen, and five seconds left. I don't know what I supposed to do with that information. Did they want me to start talking like the Chipmunks if I was going to go over? Or drag every word out if I had extra time? I was going to finish my joke no matter what. I couldn't be in the middle of a set up when the five-second card came up and just go, "Ahhhh, forget that story. Thank you!"

After I finished, bowed, and thanked the audience, I headed offstage. By the time I changed my clothes, the studio was empty. Denise and I looked around, but we were the only ones left. We returned to the dressing room and grabbed our stuff. I received a gift bag to take home. Inside was a *The Late Late Show with Craig Ferguson* T-shirt, a bottle of Captain Morgan, and a card signed by Craig that said THANKS. The town car took us home. I still had a couple of days to ease off the cleanse, so we couldn't celebrate that night. We decided to wait till we found out the air date.

A week later Celia called to say that my segment would air that Friday; I was relieved. But I wouldn't be at home that night. I had a show with my friend Don Friesen in northern California. It was just one show that night, a benefit at a school. It would be over by 10:00 PM and *Ferguson* didn't come on until 12:30. I hoped there was a way we could catch it. I was Tivo-ing it, but wanted to see it air live, too.

Don asked me on the way up if I wouldn't mind driving back to L.A. after the benefit. The hotel room wouldn't be comped. I'd rather pocket more money, so I agreed to head back right after.

I opened the show and then brought Don up. While he was onstage, my friend Dave Loughman from the Navy called me. When I picked up he was screaming into the phone, "You're on TV! Misty and I are watching you right now! What's up with that Willy Wonka jacket?!"

After the show, Don and I started the five-hour drive home. We were lost in conversation when I looked at my watch and saw that it was 1:00 AM. I asked Don if we could get off at the next exit and see if there was a bar or something we could try to watch my set as it aired on the west coast. He said, "Of course."

The I-5 connects Sacramento and Los Angeles. And nothing else. There are lots of exits, but most of them are there only because of the highway and lead to fast food places, gas stations, and sometimes hotels. We thought it might be possible to go to a hotel and see if they had a TV in the lobby. But it was late, and every hotel's lobby we went to was locked. We checked out a few restaurants, but by then they were either closed or had no TV.

We gave up our search and headed to a gas station to get gas. I went inside to use the bathroom and saw signs that said TRUCK-ERS LOUNGE. That sounded promising. It was only 1:28 AM. The late-night shows begin and end at thirty-five minutes after the hour, so I thought there was still time. I ran down the hall to the lounge. It was wide open with lots of couches and an old giant rear-projection television in front. Some bad movie was on and one trucker was sleeping in the back. I hurried to the TV and tried to figure out how to change the channel. I found a button on the back, but that changed the "source" and the screen went to fuzz. This woke up the trucker, who groaned a bit. I gave a pre-emptive apology, "Sorry. I'm trying to find CBS. I'm on there."

The trucker acted like this was a normal occurrence and said, "Ya gotta use this remote," and held one up. I grabbed it from him. I started flipping around. NBC, check. ABC, check. Home Shopping Network, check. CBS, nope.

Don finally came in and we flipped through all the stations together to confirm it wasn't on. By this time the show would have been almost over anyway, so we gave up. I returned the remote to the trucker and we hit the road. I missed my own television debut.

29

On a Roll?

Finally a terrific year! Despite the fact that 2007 began without a single word from Eddie Brill about the second DVD I sent him in December, the new year was still off to a great start. I had another round of scans and lab work in March, and the results showed my tumors hadn't grown. In fact, my oncologist said that it looked like one them may have even shrunk a little. That was fantastic news.

Money was still super tight, but I had a lot of comedy work lined up and Denise's studio was finding its footing. All of this, combined with my stable health, gave me confidence about my dream, too. I had made my television debut on a show that aired immediately following Dave's show. Denise and I decided there would be no better time to start trying to have kids, so 2007 would be the year.

With all that I had accomplished, I felt like I was getting closer to *Letterman*. But Eddie never responded to the second DVD I sent. I wasn't sure it had even made it to his desk. I sent another DVD in case it got lost in all the holiday mail, but I didn't hear word about that one either. The odds of two DVDs getting lost in the mail were pretty low, so I figured he just didn't like what I had sent.

So I got back to work coming up with a new five-minute set to send him. It took a few months to work it out, and another couple to capture it on DVD. I sent it out immediately. I heard nothing. Soon it had been a year since I spoke with Eddie. I didn't know where I stood anymore.

The year was flying by, and that November I was booked to feature at the San Francisco Punch Line with a big-name headliner. But two weeks before the show, Molly from the Punch Line e-mailed me and told me that the headliner had canceled. I'd still be featuring, though, but this time with a new headliner. His name? Eddie Brill.

Holy crap! A whole week working with Eddie! That's six shows with him. I'd be doing twenty-five to thirty minutes a night in front of him. I could get a lifetime of DVDs and material in front of him in that week alone. I spent the two weeks leading up to the gig working on as many different sets as I could. I would show him everything I had. Surely he would find five minutes in there he liked.

He didn't. It was the most anticlimactic week of my life. Eddie was a nice and very friendly person, but I didn't feel any closer to him on Saturday than I did on Tuesday when I first met him. Usually I have lunch or dinner a couple of times with the other comics and get to know them, but for most of the week Eddie hung out with some friends he had in the city. He was busy.

I understood. But I didn't like it.

The Punch Line is basically my home club. I know it well. From the stage you can see the green room where the comics hang out. Every night I watched the green room door to see if Eddie would come out to watch my set. He came out a few times, but just to get something to eat or drink from the bar. He'd watch while he was waiting for his stuff, but there was never a purposeful pull-up-a-chair moment.

To be fair, Eddie didn't have to do that. He wasn't expected to do that. Well, I expected him to do that, but no one else did. Eddie is a comic himself, with his own pre-set regimen. He had to worry about what he was going to do that night, not what I was doing. Eddie was headlining, and the pressure was on him to send the crowd home feeling good. That is what he was being paid for. No one, not even me, was paying him to watch my set. I just wanted that. And I didn't get it.

I wasn't mad; I was disappointed. I had prepared an eclectic repertoire for no reason. On Saturday night in between shows, though, Eddie did ask his friends to leave the green room, so he and I could talk. He told me he was watching me, even though he knew I thought he wasn't. I was good but still not ready. I didn't know if he was being honest or just blowing smoke up my ass. I figured I had nothing to lose, so I brought up the DVDs I had sent him. He said he got them, but they didn't have anything worth-while on them.

Ouch. Not one joke out of two DVDs. I felt like I was moving backward. Eddie said to keep working at it and send him DVDs. Even though my confidence was shattered, I went up and killed on the second show. But with each laugh I got, I thought, *Not good enough for* Letterman.

I drove home to L.A. that night after the show. It was six hours of feeling bad about myself. I had been given a golden opportunity and came away with nothing. Driving home in the dark alone was the only place I wanted to be. To figure out what I could do next.

So 2007 had an auspicious start and its end sucked in a big way. The week with Eddie had left me dry on material that I could send him. I had to start from scratch, and without much direction. Denise's studio was struggling, too. Actually the studio income itself was growing more and more each month, but even on the good months there wasn't much extra money to pay the bills we had at home. All the money she made had to go for the bills that accrued when she opened the studio. We had a few months that my comedy money supported us completely, which scared me because comedy gigs come in waves. It's feast or famine. I was happy I was feasting, but I worried about what would happen when the studio and I had a bad month at the same time.

On top of all that, the year came to an end. Another year without getting on *Letterman*. Once again I gave myself an extension—one more year to get on the show. This extension didn't feel as encouraging as the previous one. I mean, how many extensions did I have left? I was three years into a five-year worst-case-scenario prognosis. Who knew if I was going to get another extension? The alternative would have been to give up and let the prior two years be a waste. Did all the progress I made—and I reminded myself that I did make some—have to be in vain? I decided to plow forward and figure out what I needed to do to make my dream happen. I just had no idea what that might be. Hopefully, 2008 would provide the answer.

30

Small Peaks and Big Valleys:
2008–2009

My comedy feast was coming to an end, and there was nothing down the road that looked like it could carry us. It was time to make some tough decisions.

Denise would work a second job during the day, before her studio opened; I would substitute teach when I wasn't on the road. I had taken the teaching certification exam when I first moved to California almost ten years earlier, just in case I didn't find some work in the broadcasting field right away. Luckily, I never had to use it. I found other work pretty quickly and then started doing comedy. I was proud that I never had to implement my back-up plan. Now, a decade later, I had to use it. I felt like I was going backward.

I started to have bouts of depression. Anyone who has ever been depressed knows that you don't have the most rational or productive thoughts. I second-guessed everything and had awful thoughts of regret running through my head: *If I was on my own I wouldn't have to worry about all these extra bills. I could live a much less material lifestyle than with Denise. I could have roommates; I could live in a crappy neighborhood; I could wear clothes until they were old and ripped; I could do without cable.* For years I had made sacrifices so that I could be a comedian and only a comedian, and now I was being pushed backward and I resented it.

Of course, this was all selfish. Denise had made my life better in every way. The real problem in all of this was that I had gotten sick. That I was sick. Had that never happened, Denise and I wouldn't be rich, but we'd be managing. Denise's studio would have been tough to get up and running under ideal conditions, but starting from the hole we were in because of the medical bills made it much worse. There were months when the studio did fantastic and Denise still wasn't sure that it could ever be profitable. She wanted it to be, but she didn't know if it could be. She could schedule only so many classes, and only a fixed number of people could fit in those classes. Still, Denise's studio was her *Letterman* and we had to find a way to make it work.

The situation was incredibly stressful on us both and, therefore, on our relationship. We both resented the other a little for having to get second jobs. Denise, I'm sure for having to deal with all my medical bills that dragged us down every month and didn't allow her to just focus on her business. I was holding a grudge that I was being forced to take a job I never would have if I were on my own, or if she hadn't opened the studio.

Deep down we both knew that the other had made extreme sacrifices for the other's dream. But you seldom act on the feelings deep down. You act on the fear-based ones that are on the surface. Thankfully through all the bad feelings and fights about money and what we had to do to make it work, those deeper feelings prevailed. They kept us from making any rash decisions about giving up on each other or our dreams.

Even with the second jobs, it became obvious that we were keeping up with only our monthly bills. We were making little or no dent in the medical bills. All of our credit cards were maxed out, and bill collectors were calling day and night. Most of our accounts had been handed over to agencies who were threatening legal action.

Part of me considered just quitting comedy and looking for a normal job with benefits. But I just couldn't do it. If I had only a couple of years left, I couldn't imagine spending them doing the opposite of what I wanted, just so I could be debt free by the time I died. It was no way to spend the rest of my life.

By the end of the first year after I received my diagnosis, Denise had brought up filing for bankruptcy. I said no. I was confident that somehow I would be able to pay all those bills. But a year and a half later, I realized she was right. We were only getting farther behind. We owed over $60,000 in medical bills, and they would continue to pile up. We saw no other option than to file.

I did research to make sure that if we declared bankruptcy it wouldn't affect Denise's studio. It wouldn't. That step seemed silly at some point, too, because the bills at her studio were a big drain on us as well, but we wanted to make her dream work. Over a period of a few months, we filed the papers, visited the lawyers, gathered information, and went to court. It wasn't easy. But I was surprised how emotionally difficult filing for Chapter 11 was.

How good of a comedian could I be if I couldn't pay my bills? I wasn't a new comic; I had been doing it for a decade and still couldn't handle the expenses involved with living. Maybe I was in the wrong line of work. By making a living at comedy full time,

I was already in the top 25 percent of all comedians, but that success meant nothing if I couldn't pay my bills. You could either get by or not. Right now I couldn't. The financial problems combined with the lack of any progress on the *Letterman* front left me in a bad place.

In February of 2008, just when I felt my lowest about comedy, I received a gift. Celia from *Craig Ferguson* called and said they had an unexpected slot to fill. Could I be ready to do a spot by Tuesday? I obviously had several five-minute sets in my pocket, so I told her I could definitely do it. Celia asked me to immediately send her the set I planned to do, which I did. She loved it. I was a go.

This time I felt much more comfortable than I did the first time. I knew what to expect from being in front of the cameras and where to look and focus. Lee and Denise both came. I could hear them laughing in the back of the audience. That made me relax, too. I had a really good set.

Timing is everything, and the timing for this second television appearance couldn't have come at a better time. It helped break me out of my funk and renewed my faith in my ability and career. I substitute taught at the grade school the day before the taping and the day after, which was a little humbling, but it still felt great to have another TV appearance under my belt; my new attitude also gave me enough energy to get back to work on new material to send to Eddie.

I'd substitute teach during the day, and then come home and write new material. Denise's dogs, Cali and Lexie, kept me company because Denise was at the studio till 9:00 or 10:00 every night. The dachshunds were getting old and just slept all the time, but it felt good to have them next to me on the couch as I worked. I talked to the dogs and ran ideas past them. They just stared back. Sometimes I thought that was a bad sign because they didn't laugh. At other times I was happy that at least I had kept their attention. It's all in how you look at it.

I looked forward to the weeks when I had comedy gigs booked, because then I'd have to substitute for only a couple of days. I treasured those shows more than I ever had. Like most kids in grade school or middle school, there was a time when I thought about being a teacher—of history, possibly. Now that I was doing it, I knew it couldn't have been a career for me. Steve Martin described teaching as being like stand-up comedy because you have to keep the students' attention at all times. I loved that part of it—making learning fun. But there are also the kids, for whatever reason, whom you can't connect with or reach, and that frustrated me. Couple that with my position as a substitute and, well, . . . we all remember how we treated substitute teachers.

By late spring I finally had some new material for Eddie, so I sent it off. I received no response, so I got right back to work on another new set.

Denise and I were becoming discouraged on the baby front, too. We had been trying for over a year with no luck. It bothered me, but Denise was really upset. I was gone a lot, and with our busy schedules we probably weren't hitting the ideal ovulation times, but that didn't make Denise feel any better. To make things worse, several members at Denise's studio were getting pregnant or showing up with babies; it killed her to see it.

We kept trying, but it often felt like a job or just a reminder that what we were doing wasn't working. Not that I'm one to complain about sex. But it was just another thing not moving forward.

In the fall of 2008, I had another new set ready and sent it off to Eddie. This was my fifth DVD. All in all, I had probably sent him almost an hour of material, and who knows how many actual jokes. As I had in the past, I followed up with an e-mail and phone call to make sure he got it. I got no response from either.

One thing helped me through all the droughts of not hearing from Eddie: hope. As frustrated as I would get, I'd turn my focus onto the next DVD that I hoped would be the one to win Eddie over. I even had a visualization technique that I used when I worked out at the gym: on the treadmill, when I was almost to my goal, I would add an extra mile or a few more minutes. Though I'd be exhausted, I'd imagine Eddie Brill way off in the distance, opening the door of the Ed Sullivan Theatre and waving me in. I told myself that I if I didn't make it to the end, to him at the door, I would never get on *Letterman*. And if I did finish, I would. This visualization exercise helped me stay hopeful and motivated. And at a steady weight!

The high I felt after *Ferguson* had run its course, and the last nonresponse from Eddie put me back in the dumps. I was feeling more depressed than I had in my whole life. I wasn't so sure about reaching my dream anymore. Was I lying to myself about being good enough for the show? Maybe my chance to be on the show had come and gone. I got the show's and Eddie Brill's attention. They looked at me, and I still didn't get booked. Maybe I wasn't good enough and just hadn't faced it yet.

It was a relief when the year finally came to a close. It had been a tough one: We filed for bankruptcy, were unsuccessful having a baby, started working second jobs, and I made no progress with my dream. I was ready to see 2008 in my rearview mirror.

The New Year didn't start off much better. The extension of my dream to get on *Letterman* was becoming an annual ritual. It felt like a New Year's resolution you knew you would break. I also had another round of scans scheduled in mid-January that I wasn't looking forward to.

My attitude toward my goals infiltrated my feelings about the upcoming scans. I wasn't as optimistic as I had been in the past because my overall feeling was negative. I had no real reason to think everything wasn't stable. I felt as good as I had over the past few years. My only complaint was some cramps and discomfort in the area where my liver is, but I'd had that since the diagnosis. It wasn't happening any more often or feeling any worse than it had before. Still, I was sure my tests would go as bad as everything else.

Around the same time, Lee suggested I interview a great comic named Robert Schimmel, Eddie Brill's favorite comic. But Lee didn't want me to interview Schimmel for my *Letterman* quest. He wanted me to interview him because Robert Schimmel, like me, had cancer. A large part of Schimmel's act was about living with cancer, so I thought Lee's idea was a great and timely one. Perhaps Schimmel would add some depth and relevance to the documentary.

Meeting Schimmel wasn't like seeing him during one of his acts. On stage, he is brash and crass and funny as hell. But in person he is soft-spoken, unassuming, and insightful. I watched the taped interview a few times in the weeks after the night we met. He said so many things that echoed my sentiments. And in those viewings I'd watch one particular part over and over again.

My oncologist told me to embrace . . . the cancer . . . that I have. And not be afraid of it. To not give it that much power. And yes, that cancer might be a part of your life . . . but it's a *part* of your life . . .

you still control your life. And I've never let that get in the way of anything. If there's something that you're chasing, and you wanna do it, then you just have to do it.

It all hit home with me. It even made me admit something to myself: I had been using cancer as an excuse *not* to chase my dream with all my heart. It was like cancer was giving me permission to fail. I hadn't been pulling out all the stops or putting the same effort into my dream that I had been when I gave myself the original goal. I was just going through the motions again, hoping it would happen.

No one would fault me if I didn't get on the show. I had made a good effort at it. I came close. If I wanted to, I could walk away feeling good about myself, and everybody would say I did my best. But the truth was I wouldn't feel good. I hadn't been doing my best. I had been feeling sorry for myself and doing just enough to live with myself. I felt like a coward.

I took to heart what Robert said, and when my scans came back stable with no growth on the tumors, I realized that the only thing standing in my way was me. It was time to regain the passion for my dream and stop making excuses. Getting by wasn't how I wanted to spend my life. I was going to live my dream or die trying.

Instead of giving up, I was going to make one final push to get on the show. I was going to get back into the clubs and find a great new set of jokes that fit what Eddie had told me the show was looking for. By the end of February 2009, I had a new DVD.

Except for the first ten-minute DVD I sent to Eddie, all the tapes contained five-minute sets. This time I sent him one that was nine minutes—five minutes of about eight jokes that were *Letterman*-esque (according to the feedback he had given me

years earlier), and one long joke that went on for about four minutes about hotel keys. The key joke was one long story and the
complete opposite of everything that Eddie said he was looking
for. It had characters. And it had a lot of physical humor. Truthfully I was thinking about editing it out of the DVD before sending it because it was so different from what he had ever liked.
But I started to think about what Brian Regan, Jim Gaffigan, Ray
Romano, and Kevin Nealon said to me: You have to do what you
do best . . . and hopefully the *Letterman* show will like it. I was
proud of this joke, so I just left it on the DVD and sent it.

*So my wife travels with me . . . if I'm staying at a nice hotel
. . . so she doesn't come along very much.*

*I stay at a lot of awful places. Last week I stayed at a
place that when I checked in they gave me a key . . . a key . . .
NOT a key-card*

. . . A KEY!

*I was like, [jump up and down] "Oh my God, did I just win
a car? Did I just win a car? . . . No? I didn't just win a car? . . .
What's this key for? Is this a hotel or a gas station?*

*This is my room key? I like the keychain . . . I like how you
put my room number on there . . . that way if I lose it, the person who finds it can find exactly what room I'm keeping all
my valuable stuff in . . . this is an excellent tradition you're
keeping in place.*

*Come on! Any decent place has switched over to the credit
card–swiper keys . . . and a hotel still using a key is basically
saying, [act out] "Welcome! . . . we haven't renovated in the
past thirty years . . . enjoy your stay . . . and the black-and-
white TVs."*

But I'll tell ya what. I like the key better. Ya know why?
'Cuz the key always works!... Ya never go up ten flights of
stairs with a key [act out trying to make work] No... no...
no...

The credit card–swiper thing never works for me the
first time... I've been traveling all day, I'm tired, I'm carry-
ing my bags, and I finally get to my room... [act out trying
card] Red... Red... Not gonna happen.

My wife is there, and she wants to help out. [imitate her
shaking head disapprovingly]

WIFE: *You're doing it wrong.*

ME: *What?*

WIFE: *You're doing it wrong. You don't swipe it. You drop*
it in the slot and let go.

ME: *You don't think I know how to operate a door?... You*
think if you weren't here I would just fall asleep in the hall-
way and not try anything else?

WIFE: *Just drop it in the slot and let go.*

ME: *[sigh, then act out trying and not working] Red...*
NO!

WIFE: *Okay, swipe it really fast.*

ME: *What happenned to your first idea? You're just giving*
up on that?

WIFE: *Just swipe it fast.*

ME: *[swipe several times fast—even put in holster and*
draw it fast] Nope... still red. Any other bright ideas?

WIFE: *Okay... drop it in the slot, AND THEN don't look*
at it...

ME: *What the hell are you talking about?... Why would*
it matter if I was looking at it?... [slowly attempt while

talking and looking to wife] Is it working? I can't look
at it. I can tell by the red in your eyes it's not working!

Okay, so now you have to start all over again. You have to
pick up your bags and go all the way back down to the lobby .
. . and they're never apologetic . . . they blame you.

CLERK: *It's not working? . . . Hmmmmmm. . . . Did you put
it next to something? . . . Like a magnet?*

ME: *A magnet? . . . Did you say a magnet? . . . Who do I
look like, Wile E. Coyote? . . . No, I didn't put it near a magnet.
. . . Do you have a magnet store here in the hotel? No? Then
no, I didn't put it near a magnet. . . . I had it in my wallet.*

CLERK: *Oh, you can't do that. . . . You see, your credit
cards in your wallet will demagnetize it.*

ME: *Oh, really? . . . Well you should put a little note on
here that says "Does not play well with other things that look
EXACTLY like it!"*

CLERK: *I'll recharge it. Just don't put it in your wallet or
your pocket. . . .*

ME: *My pocket, why not?*

CLERK: *Well, you probably have a phone or some change
or some other metal in your pockets, and they'll all demagnetize it.*

ME: *Well, I do need to get it up to my room somehow. . . .
Do you have one of those Star Trek beam things back there?
Maybe you could zap it up and I could meet it up there?*

CLERK: *You're just being silly now, sir. . . . I'll recharge
it, and when I hand it back to you, you just need to hold it
over your head [act out] . . . away from every other object on
planet Earth . . . and then take the elevator like you are the
Statue of Liberty . . . and when you get off . . . just walk down*

to your door and then bend over . . . drop it in the slot . . . and
don't look at it.

The set wasn't the only thing I sent to Eddie. A couple of weeks after sending the DVD, and getting no response, I sent him a pretty confrontational e-mail. Nothing mean or angry; just not as polite as the ones I had sent before.

I basically said that since I had no idea if he liked or even got any of the DVDs I had sent over the past two years, I was starting fresh. I told him that I thought these jokes were worth looking at and to please give me some feedback so I knew if I was getting any closer. I figured being nice hadn't gotten me any response, and, really, at this point what did I have to lose?

Well, whaddya know, that e-mail got a very quick response. And not a bad one, either. Eddie wrote me back, "Hey Pal. I got your DVDs and if I had any news I would have given it to you."

Okay, so he had received my DVDs and just not cared for anything on them. That was good to know, even though it hurt. Then, unbelievably, he singled out one joke he liked on the new DVD. It was the long, character-driven, physical joke about the hotel key. He said he really liked it, which felt so good to hear after three long years of his liking nothing.

Then the e-mail got interesting. Here's what he wrote after complimenting the key joke:

I want you to put it on tape for me, but end with the end of the magnet bit with the words . . . "exactly like it!" I have one tag suggestion to use a callback. . . . Say . . . "You wouldn't happen to have a door with a key?" And with your hand, mimic using a regular house key. That is the big closer of that bit. Call back to your wife is good, but not strong enough and believable enough to get a bigger laugh after the part before it.

I still like the 5/3rds insurance bit, but it might not fit.

It would be one piece about the keys. I know how to tighten it up some, but just get me a set with that bit. I wanna see how it plays alone. If I like it, I can let the producers see it.

Hope you are well,
Eddie

Wow! The producers would see it. I was getting close. I just needed to make the changes he was suggesting and send it to him. I was ecstatic. And a little worried.

Long bits like the key joke don't just come out ready to go. They take a long time to form and get right. I worked on that joke for half a year to get it to where it was when I sent it to Eddie. His suggestions were good, but I knew the ending I had was the best one for it.

I needed some advice, so I sent the e-mail to Denise. She knew the joke well and agreed that it probably wouldn't work the way he was suggesting, but what other option did I have? Gary came over, and he read the e-mail. He was really excited for me. He knew this meant I was getting close; I just had to do what Eddie asked and then leave it up to the producers. I asked Gary what he thought about the changes, and he agreed I had no choice but to try to get the joke to work the way Eddie suggested.

I immediately set up shows to work out these new changes and get a tape at the same time. But my fears were right; I couldn't get the joke to work the way he wanted. He felt that the ending was unbelievable, but everything I attempted just fell flat. I was so close, but the audience response to the changes told me I wasn't getting closer.

A month passed and I still had no tape with the joke working with the changes. I was even hoping for a fluke audience who would laugh at anything, just so I had a tape of it working once. But that never happened. I asked Lee and Cash for their help in finding ways to make it work, but we couldn't make it happen.

One morning Eddie posted on my Facebook wall:

What happened to the follow-up DVD you were supposed to get me? I am booked through July now. I thought you were dying to do *Letterman*! I called you in March and it's nearly May and I haven't heard a peep.

Was he serious? Haven't heard a peep? That's because I have been busting my dying-to-do-*Letterman* ass trying to get the joke to work how you asked for it. I didn't understand why he would call me out on my Facebook page and make it look like I was doing nothing to get on the show. I thought he was a nice guy.

I called Denise and had her read his comments. She couldn't believe it either. She was convinced there must be some miscommunication. When she got home we pulled up Eddie's original e-mail from a month earlier. "Aha," Denise said, after I read the e-mail out loud.

"What are you *aha*-ing about?"

She singled out "It would be one piece about the keys. I know how to tighten it up some, but just get me a set with that bit. I wanna see how it plays alone."

Denise said when I read it aloud she realized he wanted me to send another DVD right away. It didn't have to have the changes to show the producers. We could work on it after that, but he had wanted a DVD with just that joke, none of the ones that preceded it.

I couldn't believe it. I had been one quick edit and a stamp away from having the producers see a joke. But because I had misread his e-mail, I missed my chance.

I immediately sent Eddie a message explaining what I thought he meant in his March e-mail. I told him there would be a DVD on its way the next day. But who knew if it mattered? Weeks passed and he didn't respond to my e-mail or the DVD. Had I blown my chance after all this time because I couldn't read?

31

So Close

By the time August rolled around, it had been several months since Eddie had posted on my Facebook wall. I wasn't too worried about it. A couple of months was nothing compared to the entire year I hadn't heard from him. Plus it was summer. The show was probably not shooting as often. Who knew how much time Eddie was actually at the office and how much work he was doing on the show? He had a busy comedy career besides his *Letterman* job. I was busy, too, and that helped keep me from becoming depressed about the lack of progress. But in the back of my mind I wondered if he had shown the producers the bit and they just didn't care for it.

For a few Augusts in a row, I had been doing a non-comedy event with my friend Rich Davis, the guy who ran the Comics on Duty shows for the troops. Besides booking entertainment for the troops, Rich handles transportation for large events like the Super Bowl and awards shows. He is hired to manage all the VIP pick-ups, drop-offs, and mass movements of people that those occasions require. When Rich needs extra help with an event, he asks some of the comics he trusts to lend a hand. The money is pretty good, so if I'm not performing, I always take the work.

Rich has run the transportation for the Wyndham Championship golf tournament in Greensboro, North Carolina, for many years, and I started helping out in 2006 or 2007. Greensboro is a small Southern town with a lot of charm and great people. And for a week every August, I'd go there and drive around guest celebrities and bigwigs. Plus, when I wasn't carting VIPs around, I was hanging out with a bunch of comics and other cool people. It was always fun.

In 2009 I did the event just as I had the years preceding it. On the last day, a Monday, all the drivers met Rich to return the vehicles to the rental agency. Tom Foss, a comic whom I had toured with overseas, Rich's brother-in-law, Roger Seaver, and our buddies Mike Mahoney and Jim Watry were there. We were all in good moods because once the last of the cars was dropped off, we were headed for a round of free golf before we flew home that evening.

The rental agency was packed, and while we waited in line my phone rang. I dug in my pockets while listening to Rich's teasing about my wife calling to check up on me. When I looked at the phone, I saw Eddie Brill's name as the caller. Stunned, I showed Rich. He knew very well who Eddie Brill was. His eyes lit up. Then he yelled at me, "Don't just hold it; answer it!"

Why would I rush to answer it? I knew that Eddie was just calling to say he had received the DVD but hadn't had time to watch it. Either that or he had some "words for me." I had seen on his Facebook page that he was in Europe for a wedding the week before, so I guessed that he was just catching up on things now that he was back.

I walked out to the parking lot to answer the phone. "Hi, Eddie. Welcome back to the New World."

"It's good to be back." Eddie chuckled. "I've got some good news for you. I'm gonna put you on TV!"

I don't know when I began jumping and fist pumping, but at some point I turned and looked back at the rental car building to find my friends, like puppy dogs behind a glass window, jumping up and down, too.

Amid my excitement, I realized Eddie was still talking. I tried to calm down enough to comprehend what he was saying.

"You're not talking about a Cash-4-Gold commercial, are you?" I joked. "You mean on *Letterman*?"

"No, this is a public access show I do out of my basement," Eddie joked back.

My mind swirled. I couldn't focus. I heard every other word Eddie said, but couldn't piece it all together. Did he just say *Letterman*?

I ran that question through my head a few times before I realized Eddie was rattling off a list of instructions. Quick, pay attention!

"Pick a song to come out to."

"Wear something upscale . . . preferably a suit."

"You can have four guests come to the show."

"Someone from the show will call to arrange travel."

"Come in on a Sunday."

"You'll do the show Monday."

Monday? "As in next Monday?" I asked. This slapped me back into focus.

"Yeah. You'll fly in this Sunday. We'll run the set at a couple of clubs, and then you'll do the second show we tape on Monday."

Eddie was running a mile a minute, and the fact that my body and mind were contending with a plethora of emotions, I didn't take in much—except *Letterman* and Monday.

Eddie said not to worry because he'd be sending me an e-mail with the instructions he just gave me, including a rundown of the schedule for the next week. "Congrats, Buddy."

I forced myself to regain enough composure to give him a sincere, "Thank you, Eddie."

I hung up and hugged all the guys as they came up to congratulate me. I told them I was going to skip golf. I needed to get on an earlier flight back to Los Angeles so I could start planning my trip to New York!

Denise usually picks me up curbside at the airport. But this time she parked the car because, she said, she wanted to hug and kiss me forever. She didn't want some traffic officer telling us we had to keep moving. I got my bags and headed to where she was parked.

When I exited the parking elevator, I saw Denise standing by our car. I walked toward her and she ran to me. I dropped my bags and we hugged each other hard. We held on for a long, long time, squeezing out all the years of pressure, stress, and tension.

Denise. She had been with me every step of the way, and she'd cross the finish line with me in New York City.

32

Finish Line

Gary, Lee, Cash, and Sean, were ecstatic when I told them. It felt like a shared accomplishment from all the help and support they had given me over the years. They all asked if there was anything they could do to help me get ready. All I had planned for the five days before the show was buying a suit and running the set at as many clubs as possible.

Tuesday Denise and I went shopping for the suit. Right away Denise campaigned for a dark blue one, with light lines of green and light blue. It almost looked checkered. I was worried about it. It was funky. Kind of retro. It almost looked like something a salesman from the '50s would have worn. But it was sharp. A really expensive Hugo Boss. Denise said we could use the money I made from doing the show to pay for it. I was unsure. But in the end, I figured this was a once-in-a-lifetime opportunity; I should look as good as possible.

Debate over.

I took Lee up on his offer to help, and he accompanied me on the drive to almost every set I did that week. I think in five days I squeezed in eight sets. I ran the set everywhere I could. The

Comedy & Magic Club gave me multiple sets; Scott Channon got me three sets at his theater; I did a couple of open mics and scheduled a late Saturday set at the Icehouse in Pasadena.

After my Saturday night show in Santa Monica, Lee and I were heading out of the parking garage when I saw a text message from Denise: CALL ME RIGHT AWAY. I wondered where she was. She was supposed to be taking a redeye to New York City that night.

When Denise answered the phone, she didn't sound good. She said she was lying on the floor in our bathroom because she felt woozy and couldn't stand. She thought she was having a panic attack.

A panic attack? I was the one who should be having a panic attack. I was going to be on *Letterman* in less than forty-eight hours, and my wife wasn't going to make the flight? I tried to remain calm, but I couldn't understand what was going on. I told her I'd be right home.

Lee dropped me off at the house and rushed to the all-night drug store nearby to get a stock of flu, cold, and upset stomach medicines.

I ran into the house, calling her name. I found her still in the bathroom sitting up against the wall.

"I'm so sorry," she said, crying.

She looked terrible. She was pale with tears running down her face. I felt like such a jerk for worrying more about the show than her. It was hard to know what to do. Denise said she just felt awful and there was no way she could get on a plane. By this time it didn't matter, since her plane was boarding anyway. I got her a cold washcloth, put it on her forehead, and put her into bed. I called the airline and they were able to switch her to an early morning flight. For a fee, of course. Denise said she thought she'd feel better by then.

The next morning Denise wasn't any better. I felt bad for her. I know she didn't feel well, but I also thought that if the roles were reversed I would've been on that plane. I've taken many plane rides feeling like crap. I wanted to say, "Suck it up and get on that plane."

But I couldn't. Denise had done and sacrificed so much for me over the years. She loved me. If she said she was too sick to get on the plane, I'd have to believe her. She wanted to be in New York, and I really needed her there for me. Our dream was coming true and she wasn't going to be there to share it with me?

We switched Denise's plane ticket again for the red-eye that night. She'd arrive the Monday morning I was going to be on the show. I got on my flight, not knowing what would happen.

I slept most of my plane ride out. It felt good to rest a little. It was exciting to be in New York. Even at the airport. It was the last day of August, the sun was shining, and the skyline looked fantastic.

I called Denise to let her know I had arrived and to find out how she was feeling. She was feeling worse. At first she thought she might have food poisoning, but now she figured it must be the flu. She had rescheduled her flight for the first one on Monday morning and wouldn't arrive until 4:00 PM, which meant a drive into the city during weekday rush hour. I had to be at the show by 5:00 PM. The timing for her to get to the theater on time would be close.

The show sent a car for me. As we drove across the bridge into the city, I remembered a story Ray Romano told me when I interviewed him. He got bumped twice from his debut appearance on the *Late Show*, once as he was on the bridge driving to the show and another time the day before he was supposed to be on.

Getting bumped, or canceled and rescheduled, is actually pretty common. It happens for a lot of reasons. Sometimes there's unexpectedly a guest who's currently in the news and is available to do the show, so he or she takes your spot. Arj told me he had been bumped twice as well. One time he found out before he left for New York, and the other he found out as soon as he landed at JFK.

It can even happen at the last second. Maybe an earlier guest in the show goes long and they just don't have time for the comedian anymore. You can be waiting in your dressing room when the producers realize there's not enough time for you. The worst story I heard was from Nick Griffin, who was right behind the curtain with the famous *Late Show* stage manager Biff Henderson. Biff handed Nick the microphone and put his hand on Nick's shoulder. He told Nick, "Don't go until I give you a nudge." Nick was nervously waiting for the nudge, when Biff pulled him backward and snatched the microphone right out of his hand. He was bumped. Nick had family in the audience waiting to see him. When he was rescheduled, none of them could make it.

Most of the time, being bumped is just an inconvenience. You still get paid, and are rescheduled as soon as possible. But I had heard rumors of a couple of comics being bumped, then falling out of the rotation and never getting on. Almost half the comics I knew who had done the show had been bumped. I was pretty lucky to have gotten this far. But there was still time to get bumped.

My driver pulled up to a cool-looking building. I had seen the name of the hotel on the itinerary the show sent me, but I didn't believe it till we were there. It was called the DREAM hotel. How fitting. It was very stylish inside. Lots of cool lighting and trendy furniture. It felt like a really big lounge. My room was small but fashionably lit in a cool blue.

The room didn't really matter because I wasn't going to spend much time there. After checking in I had time to grab a shower and a quick bite to eat before meeting Eddie. He was going to take me to a couple comedy clubs and run through the set.

I was so out of it from traveling and worrying about Denise, I don't even remember the name of the first club Eddie took me to. It was a Sunday night, so it wasn't too crowded. The host was on already, and Eddie led me backstage. I never feel comfortable the first time I perform on a new stage. Once I have shows under my belt, I feel relaxed, but never the first time. Now I had to contend with the fact that Eddie would be watching.

I did okay. Nothing impressive. There were only so many laughs I could have gotten from that small crowd, but I didn't get them. My hotel key joke and I didn't look like we were about to be on *Letterman*.

It was obvious Eddie wasn't any more impressed than the audience. We headed right out to Gotham Comedy Club in Chelsea. We spent the ten-minute ride over discussing the set. Eddie still wasn't sure about the close of the joke. I told him I had tried every possible ending and was positive this was the right one. Then he said he was worried about the beginning. *Oh no.*

Eddie didn't like the lead-in about my wife traveling with me to hotels. I was shocked. This set up the entire joke. I think Eddie could tell that his worries were worrying me, so he gave me some general advice: "Talk slower. You need to enunciate as much as possible. And when you do your act-outs, do it from one position.

Freeze your feet and move around at the waist. Also, do you need a microphone and stand?"

I had never done the joke without a mic and stand, but I wanted to show Eddie I had some confidence. "No I don't need a microphone and stand," I assured him. "I think it would work better without them."

"Great. They'd rather have comics just go with a lapel mic."

We walked into Gotham. Comedy Central shot a show there called *Live at Gotham,* so I was excited to be performing on that stage. I was due up right after the host, so I spent the time before the show started running through the notes Eddie had given me.

When the host took the stage, Eddie came by and asked me to try a couple of different things—a different ending and a line he had suggested in his e-mail. I agreed. The crowd was a little bigger than the previous club, but not huge. Maybe forty people. The host was really funny, but he wasn't getting much from them. Not what he deserved.

I had a much better set than earlier. The crowd liked me. Some of the punch lines still weren't hitting as hard as usual, but I was finding my footing. The changes Eddie asked me to make to the hotel key joke didn't work, though. I improvised and followed his ending with a line that led back to my original ending, which got a big laugh and allowed me to get offstage on a high note.

Eddie was complimentary about the ending. "You're right," he said. "That's a better line. You just really need to make that line hit hard. That needs to be the biggest laugh of the set. The band's gonna kick in when you finish it, so it had better be a huge laugh."

I guaranteed Eddie I would finish strong. He was leading me out of the club when he saw something going on in the basement.

The manager said there was an improv and sketch show going on. Eddie told me to wait there; he'd be right back.

Five minutes later he came back up and said, "Are you up for one more set?"

"The more the merrier," I said.

Eddie said there was a decent crowd for the sketch show and the person running it had agreed to give us five minutes. He wanted to see the joke one more time. We went downstairs and stood outside the room where the show was going on. Eddie said, "I wanna change that beginning. I want you to drop the whole thing about your wife. Just get right into talking about the hotel keys." He also told me to add a line after I asked if I won a car. He wanted me to say, "Is this for a '78 Buick?"

I didn't think the Buick line was that funny, and I was worried about getting to the hotel keys without the wife lead-in. But, again, I agreed to try it. I didn't even know if I was allowed to say no. I wanted to be on the show. If he wanted me to try something, I'd try it.

The square room where the sketch show was held had a bar along one side. Probably forty people were there, but it felt packed because the room was so small. The audience sat around the perimeter. It was like a theater in the round.

We watched some sketches from the door and then one of the performers said they had a special treat all the way from Los Angeles. They introduced me and I walked into the middle of the room. It actually felt good to be running the set without a hand-held mic and stand.

They loved me. The joke did great. From top to bottom they were roaring. Eddie and I hadn't heard the previous sketches get any laughs as big as I was getting. It was a little rocky getting started without the original beginning, but it worked. The Buick line even got a chuckle. And the ending callback I promised Eddie would work hit hard.

Eddie was really happy, and we went back upstairs to talk. He said he thought it was going to be great. He told me to lose the Buick line, it wasn't good enough. Then he suggested that in place of my old beginning, I just start by mentioning that I always stay at terrible places, and how surprised I was that the show had put me up at a nice place. This seemed like a good idea. I even suggested how it could be phrased so it could get a good laugh.

Eddie said, "Great. Change that beginning section, keep everything else the same. Remember, talk slow and enunciate, and watch your act-outs. That's it, Buddy. I gotta run. Any questions?"

"No," I lied, and we shook hands good-bye.

Wait! I did have a question. I had a bunch of them. I had enough to take us to show time the next day. My head was spinning the whole way home. I didn't get a cab right away. I just walked for a while, thinking about what had just happened. In less than twenty-four hours I would be doing a joke with changes I had never practiced before. And I would be doing it on national TV!

A good thirty seconds—10 percent—of the joke had been changed. There were two or three good laughs in there. The entire beginning had changed and I was going to run it like that for the first time on *Letterman*. This was crazy.

I hailed a cab and got back to the hotel. Denise was in no condition to console me, so I called Lee and Gary and told them how the night had unfolded. They both couldn't believe it. We commiserated and then they assured me that it would work out fine. What else could they say? Still, it felt good to hear them feign confidence. Lee even helped me rework the opening lines to max-imize the laugh out of the gate.

By the time I went to bed I wasn't confident, but I had done all I could do. I had written out the new version and ran it through a few times. I decided a good night's sleep was probably the best thing for me.

I called Denise as soon as I woke up, hoping she wouldn't pick up. She did, which meant she hadn't gotten on the early morning flight. She was still feeling weak and queasy and had a bad head-ache. I thought she sounded a little better, and she agreed that she was somewhat improved, just not enough to get on a plane.

It was hard to accept that I was talking with Denise from New York rather than having her there with me. She began to cry on the phone. She felt bad for disappointing me. I assured her it would be okay. I didn't blame her, but she blamed herself.

"You know, there's still a chance I might get bumped."

She didn't respond. We both felt the weight of that. Would that be welcome news or not? Even with Denise's not being there, and my set changing the night before, was it worth risking it all after getting so close? Was I jinxing it by even joking about it?

The rest of the morning I practiced the revised set. It was start-ing to roll off my tongue a bit easier. There's so much to comedy that involves confidence and polish. Sometimes it's easy to spot a new joke in comedians' acts just because their demeanor is dif-ferent when they break into it. Once you've told a joke over and over, it just flows out of you. I didn't know if these changes to the beginning of my set would work, but saying them over and over at least made them feel less stiff.

All in all, I had probably run that set, original and revised, about 200 times. It was less than a year old, so I had probably done it a hundred times at shows. Since finding out I was going to be on the show, I had done it for a dozen live audiences. On top of that, I ran it in the car for myself every time I drove somewhere. On the plane rides from North Carolina to L.A. and L.A. to NYC, I did it in my head over and over. And I did it at the DREAM hotel easily thirty to forty times. At five minutes apiece, that's a huge time investment. About sixteen hours of telling the same joke. But that's what I needed to do to get it to become second nature—to make it look like I was casually telling it.

Eventually I needed a break. I went to get a bite to eat. First, I wanted to make sure I had everything ready for that evening. So I pulled out my garment bag from the closet and double checked my suit. Everything looked good. I laid out my dress shoes and socks. I got my dress shirt ready. I went to pull out the new under-wear Denise had bought me . . . and they weren't there. The only ones I had were the pair I had worn the night before and the pair from the plane ride. I must have left the box of new undies back in L.A. Well, I couldn't go on national TV with dirty underwear. The nation might not know, but I would know. And somehow my mom would know. Moms sense things like that.

Joke and Biagio, who had come to New York as my guests, walked with me down to Times Square for underwear shopping and lunch. I was starting to get nervous, so I ended up not eating too much. I wanted to rehearse some more and headed back to the hotel.

I tried to take a little nap but couldn't fall asleep. I just stared at the ceiling and ran the changes in the set over and over in my head. I did a little meditation and envisioned myself walk-ing out and delivering the joke in the new way and getting a great response. I imagined Dave coming over and being really happy. I visualized Eddie, the audience, my family, Denise, Joke, and Biagio telling me that it went great.

A little after 4:00 PM, I got up, took a shower, and shaved. *Letterman* tapes two shows on Monday, and the first one was probably already underway. I had to meet Eddie at the studio at 5:00. I threw on my clothes and decided to run the set again in the mirror, practicing all my expressions. In the middle of the joke my iPhone rang. It was Eddie. I answered.

"Hey, Buddy, how ya doing?" Eddie said.

"Hey, Eddie, good. Just practicing."

"Good. Good. Why don't you head over now? Your dressing room should be free now. Don't wear your suit. Wardrobe will press it for you here. You ready to go?"

"Yes!"

I grabbed my garment bag and everything I needed and headed over. The DREAM hotel is only a few blocks from The Ed Sullivan Theater on Broadway and 52nd Street. It was so cool to walk out the front door onto the busy streets of Manhattan, carrying all my stuff and knowing that I was headed to do *Letterman*. I felt like I owned that city. Or at least like I was renting it for the afternoon. Best of all, once I turned the corner onto Broadway, I could see the blue and yellow marquee on Broadway that said *Late Show with David Letterman*.

How many DVDs had I sent to that building? How many daydreams had I dreamed about performing there? Too many to count. It felt so good to approach it, like the marquee was sucking me in like a tractor beam (that's for my *Star Wars* friends).

Joke and Biagio walked with me. We stopped out front and Joke took a couple of still shots of me in front of the sign. We eventually used one of those for the film poster and this book cover . . . made ya look!

The line for the second show was already forming. Probably a hundred people were lined up. My friend Larry "Bubbles" Brown told me that when he did *Letterman,* he went up to everyone in line and told them he was the comedian on the show that night and he'd appreciate their laughter and support. He said it made him feel comfortable taking the stage, and made the audience feel like they knew him already. In a club you get twenty, thirty, or sixty minutes to let the crowd get to know you and warm up to you. On TV you get five. Why not prime the pump a little bit?

I took Larry's idea to the next level. I brought about thirty of my CDs and handed them out to the people waiting in line. I gave one to every group, and told them they could burn the CD for everyone in their party. I told them I was making my debut on the show tonight and thanked them for sharing this big moment with me. Honestly, I don't think any of them believed me. People kept looking at the CD and then back at me like there was some catch.

Joke, Biagio, and I walked around to the alley in back of the theater where the talent entrance is. The minute I turned the corner there was cheering. Not for me. The *Late Show* was shooting a segment for one of the shows with dogs who competed by seeing who could jump farthest into a pool. It was a nuthouse. There were people everywhere. And dogs.

I muscled my way through the crowd, trying not to drop my garment bag, and approached the stage door. The security guy checked my name on a list and waved the three of us in. Once inside, an assistant producer took us back to a green room where she said we could hang out until they made sure my dressing room was available.

We settled in on some comfy couches and relaxed. Biagio grabbed a couple waters and some cookies off the catering table.

I took a bottle of water and told him to save a cookie for me for after the show. I'd heard from one of the comics I interviewed that the show had great cookies.

The three of us chatted a bit among ourselves, and then to some guy who worked for the dog food company that was sponsoring the jumping event. At some point a guy in a very flashy outfit whisked in and scoured the food table. He turned around and said hello. The minute I heard his voice I recognized him—Paul Schaefer. I didn't identify him right away because he wasn't wearing his glasses. I don't think I had ever seen him without them. It was like seeing Groucho Marx without his mustache. He looked completely different. He also made me realize where I was. I was really backstage at the *Late Show with David Letterman*. It was happening.

Eddie came in and asked if I needed anything. He had someone take my suit up to wardrobe to be steamed and pressed. They took my shoes to polish, too. Once the show started, someone would come get me for makeup and then bring me down to the stage ten minutes or so before my segment. Then Eddie said, "Oh, that reminds me, do you wanna see the stage?"

"Yes! Please."

Eddie walked me through a maze of cables and curtains until we were behind the wall where Dave does his monologue. Eddie took me to the side and showed me the area I'd walk out from, and then took me out onto the stage. The stage of The Ed Sullivan Theater. I was standing on the stage where Ed Sullivan had hosted his show for twenty-three years. The Beatles made their U.S. debut on this stage. Elvis appeared on this stage. Buddy Holly, The Doors, The Stones. Plus my comedy heroes Ray Romano, Brian Regan, Mitch Hedberg, and so many others. In just a little while, I'd join that list.

Stagehands were running around the set and a musician or two sat in the band area. The chairs were empty. No audience filled the theater yet. It was a beautiful theater. You could see every single seat in the place. The lower level was slightly raked so that onstage you were eye level with the back row. The balcony hung low and even the farthest back row seemed close. For such a big theater that seated 400, it felt cozy.

Eddie pointed out the mark on the stage where I would stand. He said to walk out to that mark and start my set. Afterward I was to wait there for Dave to come up and shake my hand. I asked if I could run through the set. He agreed, so I practiced walking onstage and ran through the entire set. When I finished, Eddie clapped and said. "It sounds good." He meant the new beginning we worked on.

"Okay, Pal, ready to go back to the green room?"

"Can I stay out here for a couple more minutes?"

Eddie smiled. "Sure."

I walked around the stage a bit. Much farther than I would ever go while performing. I studied the seats from different spots. I practiced walking out from the wings a few times. I practiced starting the set. I looked to where Dave would be sitting. I stared at the place where Paul would be standing. I wanted to get as comfortable as possible on that stage. When I walked out, I wanted it to feel like I was coming back, not arriving for the first time. This had to feel like a second home. A favorite stage.

I milked every last second I could on that stage. Just as I felt Eddie was going to call me back, I said, "Okay, I'm done."

Eddie nodded, patted me on the back, and led me back to the green room. When we went backstage we ran into Biff Henderson. Eddie introduced me as the comic who was on the show that night. I couldn't believe I was meeting Biff. I grew up watching and laughing at this guy, and now I was shaking his hand. Biff noticed my Navy T-shirt. "You in the Navy?"

"I was a while ago."

"Oh yeah, I was Army. Well, you're gonna do great tonight."

"Thanks. Thank you."

"All right, see you in a bit." He went back to work.

Eddie took me back through the maze. We stopped outside the green room. Eddie had to get ready for the show. Before he left he said, "Take your time. Go as slow as possible. This audience is the best crowd you could ever want to perform in front of. You're going to do great."

After ten or fifteen minutes, the assistant producer came back to escort us to my dressing room. We took the elevator to the third floor and followed her down a dark hallway to a small dressing room. She said there was another room at the end, but the guest band that was on that night would be in there.

The three of us went in and tried to relax. Fresh cookies were on the counter next to a gift bag. I wanted to eat them, but I had to wait. They were going to be my reward. I looked through the gift bag. *Late Show* T-shirt and a cool baseball cap. I told myself I couldn't try on the hat until after the show. Then I'd be on the team.

Over the next twenty minutes or so, things started getting louder outside my dressing room door. We heard people filing into the theater. The crew was hustling around backstage, and at some point my dressing-room neighbors showed up. The band had arrived.

There had to be a dozen people in their party. No way could their entire group fit in the dressing room, even though it was three times as big as mine, so they were spilling out into the hall-way and down toward my room. They looked like a band of hippies. I swear, I imagined them getting out of a smoky Volkswagen Bus in the alley and cramming into the elevator together. There were lots of sandals and white guys with dreads. I loved it. I lived in San Francisco for almost five years. It felt like home.

The band was making their debut on the show, too. I hadn't heard of them at the time. But let me tell you, this guy Bono and his friends . . . Okay, it wasn't U2. Their name was the Magnetic Zeros, and they have really soared since appearing on the show. In their August issue, *Rolling Stone* named them "Artist to watch in 2009."

Joke asked Biagio and me how many people we thought were in the band. We tried to guess which people were musicians and which were in the posse. But when they performed, I swear to you, every one of those people was on the stage singing, playing, or dancing. They were all the band. After their song, when Dave went over and thanked them, he made a joke about the incredible number of people. "That was great . . . everybody."

Almost as soon as I got back to the dressing room after meeting the band, my suit and shoes arrived. They looked great. Joke and Biagio excused themselves while I got dressed. The suit looked even better on. I looked sharp. I ran through my set at super speed one time. My first dress rehearsal. As I wrapped up, the show started.

It was obvious the show started because up in the corner of my room hung a TV screen that went from blank to blaring the sound of Paul Schaefer and the band. I looked up and saw the show intro I had watched for years. Hearing the announcer, Alan Coulter, say, "Dave's guests tonight . . . Neil Patrick Harris . . .

comedian Steve Mazan ... and musical guest the Magnetic Zeros ..." was nothing less than surreal.

I pulled my phone out to text Denise and saw that she had texted me: GOOD LUCK. YOU ARE GOING TO DO GREAT. I LOVE YOU.

I texted back, "I LOVE YOU TOO. CALL YOU AFTER."

I mentioned to Joke and Biagio, who were as nervous as I was, that I was worried because the show had already started and I hadn't gone to makeup yet. No sooner had I said that than the assistant producer who'd shown me to the dressing room showed up. "Steve, you ready for makeup?"

"Yeah. I was worried that I didn't have time, since the show was already going."

"No, you have plenty of time. Even as the second guest you probably have a half hour or forty minutes till your segment."

That helped me relax . . . a little. It made sense. Dave would do his monologue for five or ten minutes, then he'd go over and do a desk piece for another seven to ten minutes. After a commercial, they'd do the Top 10 List, which would be another five minutes. It would be about twenty-five minutes before they got to the first guest. Unless the first guest is a real bore, they usually do two segments of about seven minutes each. Neil Patrick Harris was definitely entertaining enough to do two segments. I watched *Letterman* religiously; I knew how the show ran. I had plenty of time.

As the makeup artist was applying my makeup, worry set in. Not about my performance. Not exactly. I stared at myself in the mirror and knew that I had to bring up a serious problem to her. I felt embarrassed about saying anything, but swallowed it and said, "Could I ask you a favor?"

"Sure, what is it?" she asked.

"Would it be possible for you to draw in some eyebrows for me?"

"Do you think I didn't notice that you don't have any?" she shot back. "I was all over that the second you walked through that door. Don't worry. I'll hook you up."

It's true. I have no eyebrows. Not thin eyebrows or even light-colored eyebrows. None. My brows are bald. If you look really, really close, you can see a few strings of blondish hair hanging out, but they don't amount to anything. If a man had that kind of hair on his head, you'd call him bald. The best I had was a bad eyebrow comb-over. The hairs that were there were embarrassing. I don't know why I don't have eyebrows. It's not like I lost them. Even in photos from when I was a kid I can't see them. My dad doesn't have much as far as eyebrows either, so maybe it's genetic. Or maybe my family is slowly mutating into a super-race of funny people without hair on their brows.

When Denise travels with me, she'll draw some on for me. If I'm traveling alone, I don't attempt it myself because I draw them on too thick and look like Groucho Marx. No one seems to notice until I tell them. I guess I have the kind of face that works well without them. I'm a little self-conscious about it only because I think big eyebrows are valuable for comedy. John Belushi and Jack Black made their careers using their eyebrows. You can say so much with just a lift of a brow.

As a bonus I got some extra hair, too! While the woman was doing my eyebrows, another asked if I would be bending over or ducking my head at any point.

"As a matter of fact, yes. Why?"

"Standing behind you, I see that although you don't have a bald spot, your hair is thinner in back. The lighting onstage will show that up. Unless you bend over, no one will notice."

She then sprayed something on my crown. It made it look like I had a bunch of hair up there.

Sufficiently hairy and back in my dressing room, I gulped down another bottle of water. I wanted to keep my mouth from going dry, but I didn't want to pee my pants on national TV, either. I looked up at the TV and saw that Neil Patrick Harris was walking out on stage. Less than two segments to go. I was the next guest. My mouth immediately dried up. I cracked another bottle of water.

Right after NPH (as the cool kids call him) sat down, the assistant producer popped in and said it was time to head backstage. Joke and Biagio both gave me a hug and wished me good luck. I told them I'd see them soon. I brought an extra bottle of water down with me.

The assistant producer and I took the elevator down to the first floor. I ran the beginning of the set over in my mind the whole time. If I could get the new beginning out smoothly and moved into the old part of the joke, I'd be fine. She led me through the maze, to the wings of the stage, and told me to wait there for Biff. She wished me good luck and left me alone.

Perfect. I was alone. I could do my super quick shadowboxing to get out of breath and release some nerves. I threw a few air punches and then heard Biff whisper behind me, "Don't hurt yourself."

I let out a big exhale and took a sip of water. I could hear Dave and Neil Patrick Harris talking on the other side of the set. It was pretty cool. Neil was doing great. The crowd loved him. He wore a really nice slim black suit, and Dave was teasing him that he looked like a chauffeur. Neil was giving it right back and the crowd was eating it up.

Biff came up during break and asked what I did in the Navy. I told him I was a mechanic on a submarine. He asked a few questions about that and we joked back and forth about the services a little. Then he heard something in his earphones, raised his hand, and said, "Here we go." With that he walked out to the stage for the commercial break.

Talking with Biff distracted me from what was about to happen. But the minute he walked away, nervousness crept back in. I jumped up and down and recited the beginning of the joke over and over.

When the show returned from the commercial, Dave and Neil were right back at it. The interview was going well. A little too well, I worried. I hoped the audience would have something left in them. After each witty remark I'd think, *Okay, Doogie, save something for me.*

I'm 100 percent positive Neil Patrick Harris doesn't like to be referred to as Doogie. But I only said it in my head, until that last paragraph where I put it in print. I'm sorry, Neil. Please forgive me. If you're reading this, contact me, and I'll refund the money you spent on this book.

Dave brought up some magazine that NPH was on, and they started a whole other topic. I started to worry that he'd go another segment, or that he'd run so long they'd cancel mine. After a couple minutes, Dave finally thanked Neil for being there, and said, "We'll be right back."

Gulp. Right back? Take your time. What's the rush? I was jumping around and shaking my arms out when Neil walked backstage. Biff called for him to wait so they could get his mic off of him.

I walked up to Neil. "Hey, Neil, Steve Mazan, the comedian who's next. Great job."

"Oh, thanks, man. Have fun." He smiled, we shook hands, and he walked away.

Paul Schaeffer's band was rocking out on the stage. They're so loud and so good. The music was pumping me up now. I was getting more excited than nervous. Biff came over and called one minute to go. He told me he was going to put his hand on my shoulder and I was not to go when Dave introduced me. I had to wait until he gave me a push. I waited at the side opening to the stage. Biff was right behind me. "You're going to do great," he assured me.

Unbelievably my mind started to wander. I wasn't thinking about the new beginning to my set. I started thinking about all the people I wanted to knock it out of the park for. All the people who had written me e-mails over the years, telling me I inspired them. All the people who answered my original campaign and sent the show messages demanding "Book Mazan." All the people at comedy clubs who told me I'd make it someday. All the people who shared the same dream but were told they couldn't be on.

I was even doing it for people at the *Late Show*. Annette G, who is the travel coordinator, sent me an e-mail saying that a lot of the staff had been rooting for me for a long time to get on. She said that even though their jobs are done by the time the show tapes, they were going to stick around to see my appearance that day. I wanted to do well for all of them. I wanted to do it for my Navy friend Jeff, and all the other people I had known who passed away, who had dreams they could no longer chase.

You might think the weight of all those people on my shoulders would create more anxiety. The opposite is true. Instead, I felt like I wasn't walking out on that stage alone. I had thousands of friends, family, fans, and even strangers going out there with me. It made me feel strong. It made me feel like they all believed I was going to do well, and that it would be an insult to second-guess them.

The band died down and Dave started my introduction. Biff's hand held my shoulder tight. Dave started my introduction.

"Ladies and gentleman, our next guest is a very, very funny gentleman, and I'm very happy you're in a good mood because he's making his debut with us tonight."

Good so far. Stay loose.

"He's a stand-up comedian, and he'll be performing at a place called Wiseguys in Salt Lake City. You know there is no bigger hotbed of wiseguys than there is in Salt Lake City."

The crowd cracked up.

"Hey, whaddya got caffeine in that Diet Coke?" Dave continued. "Huh? Huh? Huh?"

They were roaring now.

To show how much Eddie can read Dave's personality, when I told Eddie that's what I wanted for my introduction, he asked if I had a different set of dates to plug. He asked if I had anything in Chicago, L.A., or San Francisco. I said that was the club date I wanted to plug. The owner of Wiseguys, Keith Stubbs, gave me my first week headlining at a club. And he did it without my asking him for it. Keith saw me perform, liked it, and took a chance on me. He'd been headlining me for years, and it helped me to start headlining other places. No matter how silly it sounded to Dave and Eddie, that was the club I wanted to mention.

Dave kept poking fun of Utah. The crowd loved it, and I thought it was really funny, too. That's why I loved Dave. My only worry was that he had been riffing on the intro for a minute and a half already, and he might eat up all the time in my segment if he didn't stop. How bad would that be? Get this far and get bumped because of the intro you gave them?

Eventually Dave let the crowd die down, and said those magic words I had been waiting my whole life to hear, "Ladies and gentleman, please welcome Steve Mazan."

Paul and the band kicked into a song I had requested from my favorite band, AC/DC. I thought it was appropriate to come out to "It's a Long Way to the Top If You Wanna Rock 'n' Roll." It had been a very long way. And I was ready to rock 'n' roll.

I walked out onto that stage as confident as I have ever walked out onto a stage. Not more confident, but as confident. I don't know what it was, but the minute Dave said my name and I heard the crowd welcoming me my nervousness slipped away.

I get nervous at coffee shops where I go to to practice comedy sometimes. I never know if I'm going to be tense or have a knot in my stomach when I take the stage at clubs. I've never been able to figure out when or why I'm nervous or calm. For whatever reason, that day I was calm.

As I walked out, I paused for a brief second, looked over at Dave, and gave him a bow of respect. Then I hit my mark and raised my arm in thanks to the crowd. I could see the entire audience. The cameras were so unobtrusive that I felt like I was in a great comedy theater instead of a television studio.

The applause slowly died. I began the set and knew I had the crowd right away. They were laughing at little faces I was making in the set-up lines. The eyebrows were working. Eddie's changes were working.

The new beginning went well. By the time I got to my original parts, I was rolling. I even got an applause break on a switch I made the past week, when I changed "black-and-white TV" to "typewriter." While they were clapping, I almost started laughing myself because the next line was an even bigger hitter. When I dropped it, they roared and went into another applause break. It was incredible.

I was talking slow, as Eddie had suggested, and it was paying off. But between my going so slow and the audience applauding so much, I was worried that I'd go way over my allotted time. If Biff or someone else gave me the signal to shorten or wrap it up, I didn't know what I'd do.

I wasn't doing a series of jokes. I was doing one long bit. It was all on one topic. It had a lot of laughs along the way, but it lead to a big conclusion. I couldn't stop in the middle. It wouldn't make any sense.

My only choice was to hope I didn't get that signal, and if I did, just ignore it. I had to do what I came there to do. If they wanted to mess with it later they could. But there was no way I was going to try to shift gears mid-set and improvise an ending.

Luckily I didn't have to. Despite getting more applause breaks along the way, they never let me know they were worried about time. So I kept going slow and savoring every laugh. There was one point in the middle of the set that I actually tried to calm the audience down so I could get to the next line. It's a good complaint to have, but their praise was throwing off my rhythm! In that moment I felt like I was hosting the show for a second. I felt like Dave. I had a silly cockiness to my attitude like, "Okay, people, we have a lot of show left here, so calm down." When I see the set now, that's the part I watch over and over.

I remember a couple of things about doing the set. One is that I heard the band laughing a bunch. That's always a good sign. They see a lot of acts. I also remember some laughter from my left, but I'm not sure who it was from. That's where Dave was, but I couldn't tell if it was him. The other thing I recall is taking in that whole beautiful theater and not wanting to end. I wanted to go right past my closer and tell every joke I had ever written.

In the end, my joke that had been clocking in at four and a half minutes, was over six. As I promised Eddie, the callback I finished the set with got the biggest response. The audience roared and then Paul and the band joined in. I felt triumphant. I basked in the applause like sunlight. I raised both my hands like Rocky, and I even gave a small bow to the audience. I don't know what kept Dave from coming up to greet me. I didn't want to turn and look for him. That would be awkward. So I just kept waving thanks to the crowd.

Finally Dave came up and motioned to me. "Steve Mazan, ladies and gentleman."

The next line Dave said was very important to me. As a fan of Dave's since I was twelve, I had seen him thank hundreds and hundreds of performers. I was convinced I knew when Dave really liked someone. My theory is that you can tell by what he says to the guest when he approaches him. For example, if he says, "They loved you," or "Thanks for being here," that was more about the audience or the polish of the performance itself. Sometimes he just says the person's name a couple times. But if he says, "I really enjoyed that," or "Hilarious," that was Dave saying *he* liked it. Well, that's my theory from watching all these years anyway . . .

Dave gave me a "Great job" and a "Very funny." Icing on the cake. I was standing onstage at the Ed Sullivan Theater next to David Letterman, who had just complimented me. Few dreams ever live up to your expectations. Far fewer ever exceed them. This was one of those.

Dave announced that the show would be right back. The on-air lights went off, and he shook my hand one more time and said, "Very funny," again.

As Dave walked away, Eddie ran up pumping his fist in victory. "You did it! That was fantastic." He grabbed me in a hug.

The second Eddie let go and walked away, it all sank in. I had made it. I had done it. I had nailed it. I ran to the elevators and hit the UP button. I saw that it was on the top floor. I had too much energy to wait for it to move down. I spotted the stairs and started running up them. My dress shoes were slipping all over the place, but I kept climbing.

I got about halfway up when I heard someone below yell, "Steve!"

It was the assistant producer who had led me around earlier. "There's an elevator!"

"I'm too excited," I yelled back. "I can't wait." I was sweating when I left stage, but by the time I got back to my dressing room, I was sopping wet. I ran down the hall and swung the door open. Biagio had the camera out, and I screamed, "Yes!"

I raised my arms in victory and despite the camera, I tried to hug Biagio and then Joke. When I hugged Joke, I noticed she had something in her hand. I also realized neither of them were talking. Joke held up her phone and on the screen it showed that Denise was on the line. I grabbed it.

"Baby, it went great."

"I know; I heard," Denise said.

For a second I was disappointed that Joke and Biagio would spoil my news by telling Denise. "Oh, did they tell you?"

"No. I heard the set. Five applause breaks!"

I was confused. "What? How did you hear it?"

"Joke and Biagio held the phone up to the TV set in your dressing room. I heard the whole thing baby. You did amazing."

After twenty minutes or so, when the show was over, Eddie met us and we all went down to the stage. My mom and Gary were there, and we took photos with Eddie and each other. We easily stayed for half an hour taking it all in. I've never seen my mom smile so big.

While we were taking photos, I saw Alan Coulter, the announcer, striding across the back of the stage. He looked over and saw us all taking pictures. He changed direction, came right to me, and extended his hand. I shook it.

"That was hilarious, Steve. Great job." Then before walking away he said, "See you next time."

Next time?

WHAT ARE YOU DYING TO DO?

Acknowledgments

Thank YOU for picking up this book. Thank you to my wife, Denise, for pushing me when the writing got tough. Thanks to Michele Matrisciani for her support, patience, and incredible eye for what works and what doesn't. Thanks to Joke and Biagio for helping document my journey and for their offer in the beginning to help in any way. Thanks to my mom, sister, and Cash Levy for their feedback on early long drafts. And, finally, thanks to Drake and Hazel Witham and Sean Robinson for their encouragement, advice, and belief that I could complete this book even when I wasn't so sure.

These thanks are limited to the people who helped with this book. If I were to attempt to compile a list of those who helped me to reach my dream, I would have another book. You know who you are, and I will remind you personally every chance I get.

About the Author

STEVE MAZAN. Man? Myth? Legend? Some say none of these. He is, however, a stand-up comic. With influences ranging from Richard Pryor to Fozzie Bear, Steve has formed a unique style that bridges the gap between clever and goofy. His material offers layers that leave an audience howling and thinking at the same time. He is smart and silly. Daft and thoughtful. Intelligent and ridiculous, but always clever. And clean. Mostly.

In the decade since starting in the great San Francisco comedy scene, Steve has played clubs, colleges, and corporate events across America. In addition to reaching his dream of performing on David Letterman's show, he's been a repeat guest on *The Late*

Late Show with Craig Ferguson, Byron Allen, and *The Bob and Tom Show*.

But of all the shows Steve has done, he remains most proud of the many trips he's made to the Middle East to perform for our troops. As a former Navy submariner, Steve knows how much those men and women sacrifice for our country, how much they need our support, and how much they need someone to laugh at.

Steve lives in Los Angeles with his wife, Denise, and his dogs, Wrigley and Kuma, and currently travels the country to film festivals where his documentary is racking up critic awards and audience acclaim. For more information on the movie *Dying to Do Letterman* and about Steve, visit www.stevemazan.com and www.dyingtodoletterman.com.

Want to Book Steve?

For speaking engagements and comedy shows, email Steve at steve@stevemazan.com. You can also find him on Facebook at facebook.com/steve.mazan and on Twitter @Steve_Mazan.

Dying to Do Letterman
is also a critically acclaimed documentary!

The Reviews Are In

"Wife-and-husband team Joke Fincioen and Biagio Messina record Mazan's journey, following him as he tries to craft the perfect routine—with advice from famous funnymen like Ray Romano and Kevin Nealon—while trying to stay healthy and navigate the decidedly unfunny health care system. The result is a nimble, uplifting film that celebrates life, love, and friendship. Best of all, it's a riot."

—*The Plain Dealer*

★ ★ ★ ★

"Sidesplittingly funny . . . Shades of Rocky . . . you'll treasure every moment of it."

—*Steve Rhodes, InternetReviews*

"If we came to Cinequest to see just one film this year, THIS IS IT. The humbling, inspiring and hilarious story of a man who dared to dream big, *Dying to Do Letterman* will undoubtedly be in a theater near you (or at the very least in your Netflix queue) and soon. Told without pretense, raw, emotional, and laugh-out-loud funny (he is after all, a nationally renowned comedian), *Dying to Do Letterman* is the story of the underdog. It's a story of the everyday guy trying to seek happiness and fulfillment in life."

—*Directors Live*

**To find out how you can see this
award-winning documentary at a theater near you,
on DVD, or video on demand, please visit
www.dyingtodoletterman.com
or steve@steve.mazan.com**